Vasco da Gama
and the Portuguese Explorers

WORLD EXPLORERS

Vasco da Gama
and the Portuguese Explorers

Rebecca Stefoff

Introductory Essay by Michael Collins

CHELSEA HOUSE PUBLISHERS

New York • Philadelphia

On the cover Map of the world; portrait of Gama from a 17th-century Portuguese manuscript

Chelsea House Publishers
Editor-in-Chief Richard S. Papale
Managing Editor Karyn Gullen Browne
Copy Chief Philip Koslow
Picture Editor Adrian G. Allen
Art Director Nora Wertz
Manufacturing Director Gerald Levine
Systems Manager Lindsey Ottman
Production Coordinator Marie Claire Cebrián-Ume

World Explorers
Senior Editor Sean Dolan

Staff for VASCO DA GAMA AND THE PORTUGUESE EXPLORERS
Copy Editor Danielle Janusz
Editorial Assistant Robert Kimball Green
Picture Researcher Nisa Rauschenberg
Senior Designer Basia Niemczyc

5 7 9 8 6

Library of Congress Cataloging-in-Publication Data

Stefoff, Rebecca.
Vasco da Gama and the Portuguese Explorers/by Rebecca Stefoff; introductory essay by Michael Collins.
    p. cm.—(World Explorers)
Includes bibliographical references and index.
Summary: Discusses the travels of Vasco da Gama and other Portuguese explorers who helped establish an extensive empire for their country.
ISBN 0-7910-1303-0
    0-7910-1526-2 (pbk.)
1. Gama, Vasco da, 1469–1524—Juvenile literature. 2. Discoveries (in geography)—Portuguese—Juvenile literature. 3. Portuguese in India—Juvenile literature. 4. Portugal—History—Period of discoveries, 1385–1580—Juvenile literature. [1. Gama, Vasco da, 1469–1524. 2. Explorers. 3. Portugal—History—Period of discoveries, 1385–1580.] I. Title. II. Series.   92-14272
G282.S75 1992   CIP
910'.92—dc20   .   AC
[B]

CONTENTS

WORLD EXPLORERS

THE EARLY EXPLORERS

Herodotus and the Explorers of the Classical Age
Marco Polo and the Medieval Explorers
The Viking Explorers

THE FIRST GREAT AGE OF DISCOVERY

Jacques Cartier, Samuel de Champlain, and the Explorers of Canada
Christopher Columbus and the First Voyages to the New World
From Coronado to Escalante: The Explorers of the Spanish Southwest
Hernando de Soto and the Explorers of the American South
Sir Francis Drake and the Struggle for an Ocean Empire
Vasco da Gama and the Portuguese Explorers
La Salle and the Explorers of the Mississippi
Ferdinand Magellan and the Discovery of the World Ocean
Pizarro, Orellana, and the Exploration of the Amazon
The Search for the Northwest Passage
Giovanni da Verrazano and the Explorers of the Atlantic Coast

THE SECOND GREAT AGE OF DISCOVERY

Roald Amundsen and the Quest for the South Pole
Daniel Boone and the Opening of the Ohio Country
Captain James Cook and the Explorers of the Pacific
The Explorers of Alaska
John Charles Frémont and the Great Western Reconnaissance
Alexander von Humboldt, Colossus of Exploration
Lewis and Clark and the Route to the Pacific
Alexander Mackenzie and the Explorers of Canada
Robert Peary and the Quest for the North Pole
Zebulon Pike and the Explorers of the American Southwest
John Wesley Powell and the Great Surveys of the American West
Jedediah Smith and the Mountain Men of the American West
Henry Stanley and the European Explorers of Africa
Lt. Charles Wilkes and the Great U.S. Exploring Expedition

THE THIRD GREAT AGE OF DISCOVERY

Apollo to the Moon
The Explorers of the Undersea World
The First Men in Space
The Mission to Mars and Beyond
Probing Deep Space

CHELSEA HOUSE PUBLISHERS

Into the Unknown

Michael Collins

It is difficult to define most eras in history with any precision, but not so the space age. On October 4, 1957, it burst on us with little warning when the Soviet Union launched *Sputnik*, a 184-pound cannonball that circled the globe once every 96 minutes. Less than 4 years later, the Soviets followed this first primitive satellite with the flight of Yuri Gagarin, a 27-year-old fighter pilot who became the first human to orbit the earth. The Soviet Union's success prompted President John F. Kennedy to decide that the United States should "land a man on the moon and return him safely to earth" before the end of the 1960s. We now had not only a space age but a space race.

I was born in 1930, exactly the right time to allow me to participate in Project Apollo, as the U.S. lunar program came to be known. As a young man growing up, I often found myself too young to do the things I wanted—or suddenly too old, as if someone had turned a switch at midnight. But for Apollo, 1930 was the perfect year to be born, and I was very lucky. In 1966 I enjoyed circling the earth for three days, and in 1969 I flew to the moon and laughed at the sight of the tiny earth, which I could cover with my thumbnail.

How the early explorers would have loved the view from space! With one glance Christopher Columbus could have plotted his course and reassured his crew that the world was indeed round. In 90 minutes Magellan could have looked down at every port of call in the *Victoria*'s three-year circumnavigation of the globe. Given a chance to map their route from orbit, Lewis and Clark could have told President Jefferson that there was no easy Northwest Passage but that a continent of exquisite diversity awaited their scrutiny.

In a physical sense, we have already gone to most places that we can. That is not to say that there are not new adventures awaiting us in the sea or on the red plains of Mars, but more important than reaching new places will be understanding those we have already visited. There are vital gaps in our understanding of how our planet works as an ecosystem and how our planet fits into the infinite order of the universe. The next great age may well be the age of assimilation, in which we use microscope and telescope to evaluate what we have discovered and put that knowledge to use. The adventure of being first to reach may be replaced by the satisfaction of being first to grasp. Surely that is a form of exploration as vital to our well-being, and perhaps even survival, as the distinction of being the first to explore a specific geographical area.

The explorers whose stories are told in the books of this series did not just sail perilous seas, scale rugged mountains, traverse blistering deserts, dive to the depths of the ocean, or land on the moon. Their voyages and expeditions were journeys of mind as much as of time and distance, through which they—and all of mankind—were able to reach a greater understanding of our universe. That challenge remains, for all of us. The imperative is to see, to understand, to develop knowledge that others can use, to help nurture this planet that sustains us all. Perhaps being born in 1975 will be as lucky for a new generation of explorer as being born in 1930 was for Neil Armstrong, Buzz Aldrin, and Mike Collins.

The Reader's Journey

William H. Goetzmann

This volume is one of a series that takes us with the great explorers of the ages on bold journeys over the oceans and the continents and into outer space. As we travel along with these imaginative and creative journeyers, we share their adventures and their knowledge. We also get a glimpse of that mysterious and inextinguishable fire that burned in the breast of men such as Magellan and Columbus—the fire that has propelled all those throughout the ages who have been driven to leave behind family and friends for a voyage into the unknown.

No one has satisfactorily explained the urge to explore, the drive to go to the "back of beyond." It is certain that it has been present in man almost since he began walking erect and first ventured across the African savannas. Sparks from that same fire fueled the transoceanic explorers of the Ice Age, who led their people across the vast plain that formed a land bridge between Asia and North America, and the astronauts and scientists who determined that man must reach the moon.

Besides an element of adventure, all exploration involves an element of mystery. We must not confuse exploration with discovery. Exploration is a purposeful human activity—a search for something. Discovery may be the end result of that search; it may also be an accident, as when Columbus found a whole new world while searching for the Indies. Often, the explorer may not even realize the full significance of what he has discovered, as was the case with Columbus. Exploration, on the other hand, is the product of a cultural or individual curiosity; it is a unique process that has enabled mankind to know and understand the world's oceans, continents, and polar regions. It is at the heart of scientific thinking. One of its most significant aspects is that it teaches people to ask the right questions; by doing so, it forces us to reevaluate what we think we know and understand. Thus knowledge progresses, and we are driven constantly to a new awareness and appreciation of the universe in all its infinite variety.

The motivation for exploration is not always pure. In his fascination with the new, man often forgets that others have been there before him. For example, the popular notion of the discovery of America overlooks the complex Indian civilizations that had existed there for thousands of years before the arrival of Europeans. Man's desire for conquest, riches, and fame is often linked inextricably with his quest for the unknown, but a story that touches so closely on the human essence must of necessity treat war as well as peace, avarice with generosity, both pride and humility, frailty and greatness. The story of exploration is above all a story of humanity and of man's understanding of his place in the universe.

The WORLD EXPLORERS series has been divided into four sections. The first treats the explorers of the ancient world, the Viking explorers of the 9th through the 11th centuries, and Marco Polo and the medieval explorers. The rest of the series is divided into three great ages of exploration. The first is the era of Columbus and Magellan: the period spanning the 15th and 16th centuries, which saw the discovery and exploration of the New World and the world ocean. The second might be called the age of science and imperialism, the era made possible by the scientific advances of the 17th century, which witnessed the discovery of the world's last two undiscovered continents, Australia and Antarctica, the mapping of all the continents and oceans, and the establishment of colonies all over the world. The third great age refers to the most ambitious quests of the 20th century—the probing of space and of the ocean's depths.

As we reach out into the darkness of outer space and other galaxies, we come to better understand how our ancestors confronted *oecumene*, or the vast earthly unknown. We learn once again the meaning of an unknown 18th-century sea captain's advice to navigators:

> And if by chance you make a landfall on the shores of another sea in a far country inhabited by savages and barbarians, remember you this: the greatest danger and the surest hope lies not with fires and arrows but in the quicksilver hearts of men.

At its core, exploration is a series of moral dramas. But it is these dramas, involving new lands, new people, and exotic ecosystems of staggering beauty, that make the explorers' stories not only moral tales but also some of the greatest adventure stories ever recorded. They represent the process of learning in its most expansive and vivid forms. We see that real life, past and present, transcends even the adventures of the starship *Enterprise*.

Don Emanuel el Feliçe
primero destenombre 14.Reÿ de Portugal.
Vixit Anno 52.obiit Añȯ 1521.

The Voyage of
Vasco da Gama

Legend has it that King Manoel I of Portugal, known as the Fortunate, swore a solemn oath at dawn on July 8, 1497. In the presence of his confessor and many witnesses, he vowed to build a new church in his capital city of Lisbon, a magnificent cathedral that would contain his own tomb and the tombs of all his royal descendants—if the Portuguese fleet that was to set sail that morning returned safely from its journey.

The fleet lay in Lisbon's sheltered harbor in the mouth of the Tagus River. Bobbing at anchor were four ships: the *São Gabriel*, the *São Rafael*, the *Berrio*, and a fourth vessel, its name unknown, that carried supplies for the other three. The men who were preparing to embark on these ships hoped to be the first Europeans to reach India by sailing around the great mysterious bulk of Africa. Their captain-major, the commander of the fleet, was a nobleman and mariner named Vasco da Gama.

Gama's exact birthdate is not known, but in 1497 he was in his thirties. The portraits of him that have survived the centuries show him with brown eyes, reddish brown hair, and a long, full beard. Events would demonstrate that as a leader he was strong, prudent, persistent, and ruthless.

The evening before the fleet sailed, the captain-major had an audience with King Manoel, who was financing the venture. Gama swore his loyalty to the king, and Manoel presented him with a silk banner bearing the emblem of

King Manoel I acceded to Portugal's throne in 1495, when he was 26 years old. He inherited so many promising enterprises from his predecessor—foremost among them Portugal's maritime ventures—that he was called the Fortunate. His reign, which lasted until 1521, coincided with what is now regarded as the golden age of his nation.

A late-16th-century engraving of the Portuguese city of Lisbon, which is situated on the north bank of the estuary of the Tagus River, 10 miles from its mouth on the Atlantic Ocean. The voyages of exploration and commerce made by Portugal's mariners helped make Lisbon one of the most important cities in Europe.

the Knights of Christ, thus giving the voyage the sanction of the Roman Catholic church and placing it under God's protection. Gama then spent the night, together with his fellow captains and 100 chosen members of the crew, praying and keeping vigil in the chapel of Our Lady of Belém, built decades earlier for the devotions of sea captains and sailors.

At dawn the mariners, each bearing a lighted candle, marched from the chapel to the harbor in a solemn, traditional procession. They were carried out in boats to the waiting ships, where the crews hauled the sails up the masts and raised the dripping anchors, and the crowd on the quays watched the fleet move off down the river toward the sea.

Gama sailed in the *São Gabriel*, the flagship. His older brother Paulo da Gama was captain of the *São Rafael*. Both of these ships were of about 100 or 120 tons burden. (The size of a ship is measured in terms of its water displacement, or cargo-carrying capacity). The *Berrio* was a smaller, more maneuverable ship of about 50 tons; its captain was Nicolão Coelho, a knight and a distant relative of King Manoel's. The 200-ton storeship was captained by Gonçalo Nunez, a comrade of Vasco da Gama's. Accounts of the expedition written in the 15th and 16th centuries give varying figures for the total number of men who set out with Gama; present-day estimates range from 118 to 170, although most scholars agree that the higher number is probably closer to the truth. At least one priest sailed with the fleet. There were also a dozen or more convicts, who were regarded as being as good as dead already and therefore could be ordered to carry out particularly dangerous tasks.

The expedition had been carefully planned over a two-year period and was outfitted with the best possible supplies. In addition to many barrels of fresh water and three years' worth of food, most of it in the form of pickled meat and hard biscuit, the fleet carried 20 bombards—medieval cannons that hurled large stone balls—and enough armor, crossbows, swords, and spears to outfit the ships' companies for combat. King Manoel's scientific advisers had provided Gama with the most up-to-date maps and geographic information they could gather. An important contribution was made by Abraham Zacuto, a Jewish astronomer and mathematician who had fled to the Portuguese court in 1492 to escape religious persecution in Spain. Zacuto gave Gama sky charts and instruments for the captain-major to use in calculating his location. The *São Gabriel* and the *São Rafael* also carried stone markers bearing the royal arms of Portugal and wooden crosses; Gama was expected to plant these in any new lands he discovered to mark the claims of the Portuguese state and the Catholic church.

Gama's plan was to sail south through the Atlantic Ocean and turn left, making his way east around southern Africa and then north and east into the Indian Ocean. The first part of the journey, although perilous, was not unprecedented: Portuguese mariners had been inching south along the coast of Africa for 70 years, so the coastal waters of West Africa were not unfamiliar, and just 10 years earlier a Portuguese expedition had managed to reach and pass the southern tip of Africa, proving that it *was* possible to sail around the continent. The real mysteries lay beyond Africa's southernmost capes. Did India really lie, as Gama and others believed, on the far side of Africa? Would he find a passage northward as far as the Arabian Sea, a region frequented by Arab merchants and not altogether unknown to Europeans? Or would he find the way blocked by unexpected land masses, impassable hazards to navigation, hostile peoples? The captain-major and many members of the crew undoubtedly shared the mingled faith and foreboding expressed by the anonymous sailor on the *São Rafael* whose *Roteiro*, or route-book, constitutes the only known firsthand account of Gama's expedition: "May God our Lord permit us to accomplish this voyage in his service!"

A week after leaving Lisbon, the fleet passed between the African coast and the Canary Islands, which lie west of present-day Morocco. The following day the ships anchored off the Terra Alta, or High Land, a portion of the African coast near the Tropic of Cancer where cliffs and hills, easily visible from the sea, served Portuguese navigators as a landmark. The men fished from the ships for a few hours and then raised sail again.

Lanterns were lit aboard each vessel at sundown so that the fleet could stay together, but on the night the ships left the Terra Alta thick fog enveloped them, and they lost sight of one another and became separated. When the sun rose, reports the author of the *Roteiro*, the *São Rafael* was alone. The captains had instructions for such emergencies, so Paulo da Gama immediately set a course for the Cape Verde Islands, which lie just off the westernmost point of Africa's great Saharan bulge, where by previous arrangement the fleet was to regroup if difficulties arose.

The *São Rafael* arrived in the Cape Verdes on July 22. The *Berrio* and the storeship were already there, but there was no sign of the flagship. The *São Gabriel* did not appear until July 26. "At ten o'clock on that day," states the *Roteiro*, "we sighted the captain-major, about five leagues ahead of us, and having got speech with him in the evening we gave expression to our joy by many times firing off our bombards and sounding our trumpets." The entire fleet made a landfall at Santiago in the Cape Verde cluster to take aboard wood, water, and fresh meat. Then Gama stood out to sea, ready to cross the equator and swing around Africa.

Based on the experiences of the scores of Portuguese mariners who had explored the African coast, Gama felt that the best way to get around the continent was not to hug the coast and work his way through thousands of miles of inshore waters, plagued by sandbars and treacherous tides, but rather to sail far out to sea in a wide, southward-trending arc. By doing so he hoped to avoid battling the powerful winds and currents that flow from south to north along Africa's west coast. Instead, he would bear south at a point far west of the coastal waters and then pick up the westerly winds and currents that sweep across the South Atlantic. These would then carry him east around Africa's tip.

The fleet left the Cape Verdes on August 3, sailing a course that carried it west and south through the Atlantic, *away* from its ultimate destination in the East. Although Gama's exact course is unknown, it is thought that at his farthest west he may have been within 600 miles of South America. Gama's boldness in venturing far out to sea, away from the familiar coastline, was justified. When at last he

The original of this portrait of Vasco da Gama hung in the Portuguese royal palace in the Malabar Coast city of Goa. Gama's expedition was at the time the longest open-sea voyage made by a European.

The São Gabriel, *the* São Rafael, *and the* Berrio *round the Cape of Good Hope. Gama's voyage would result in a shift of economic power in Europe away from the Mediterranean city-states that had previously controlled trade with the East to the ocean-going nations of western Europe.*

ordered the prows of his ships turned toward the east, the fleet was swept along by westerly winds.

The bold sailors of Portugal had not seen land since leaving the Cape Verde Islands. The days turned into weeks, then months, until, on November 4, after 93 days in the open sea, the lookouts spied land once more: the arid coast of southwestern Africa. Gama had not set his course far enough south to clear the southern tip of the continent. He was about 300 miles north of the Cape of Good Hope and had to fight his way down the final portion of the coast and around the Cape in stormy, dangerous coastal waters. Even so, his wide Atlantic arc, which covered a distance of 3,700 to 4,000 miles, had saved him an arduous in-shore journey. It was the longest open-sea voyage made by Europeans up to that time; by contrast, Columbus, on his epic first voyage to the Americas five years earlier, had spent just 36 days at sea to cover the 2,600 miles between the Canary Islands and Hispaniola.

Three days after sighting the African coast, Gama landed his ships at St. Helena Bay in present-day South Africa, where he set his men to mending the sails and scraping the hulls clean. (In the course of a voyage, a ship could accumulate several tons of barnacles and seaweed on its hull, severely slowing its rate of progress. The only solution was to beach the vessel between tides and scrape it clean.) He was still 100 miles north of the Cape of Good Hope, but his ships needed repairs after the Atlantic passage. There, a group of natives—the Khoisan, a small, brown-skinned people who were later called Hottentots by the Dutch colonists—approached the ships. According to the *Roteiro*, "The captain-major landed and showed them a variety of merchandise, with the view of finding out whether such things were to be found in their country. This merchandise included cinnamon, cloves, seed-pearls, gold, and many other things, but it was evident that they had no knowledge whatever of such articles, and they were consequently given round bells and tin rings." Another encounter, a few days later, ended in a brief fight in which Gama and several others were wounded by the natives' spears; then the Khoisan disappeared.

The fleet set sail again on November 16. Although it ran into several squalls, within a week all four ships had rounded both the Cape of Good Hope and its neighbor to the southeast, Cape Agulhas—Africa's true southernmost point—where the waters of the Atlantic Ocean mingle with those of the Indian Ocean. Once around the capes, the ships dropped anchor in Mossel Bay, where the provisions and supplies from the storeship were distributed among the other three vessels. The storeship was then scuttled; useful parts were taken by the other captains, and the remainder was destroyed.

At Mossel Bay the Portuguese were approached once more by curious natives. Relations were friendly at first: the Portuguese gave the natives bells and red caps in exchange for ivory bracelets; when the natives began dancing to the music of their flutes, Gama ordered the Portuguese to sound their trumpets, and, writes the author of the *Roteiro*, "we in the boats danced, and the captain-major did so likewise." The Portuguese purchased an ox from the natives and slaughtered it for a feast, but the festivities came to a quick end when Gama began to suspect that the natives were planning an ambush. He ordered two of the bombards fired to demonstrate the power of Portuguese weapons, and the sound of the gunpowder exploding sent the natives scattering into the bush. Before leaving Mossel Bay on December 7, Gama ordered his men to erect a stone pillar and a wooden cross on the highest point of land. Looking back as their three ships sailed out of the bay, his men could see the natives on shore rapidly taking down both the pillar and the cross. The crew and officers also saw, gamboling in the waves and lolling along the shore, an animal they had not seen before—the sea lion.

On December 10, Gama's fleet passed a stone pillar in the vicinity of the mouth of the Great Fish River, set there by

Bartolomeu Dias, the Portuguese explorer who had earlier rounded the Cape of Good Hope. It marked the farthest point reached by a Portuguese mariner. Once they passed it, Gama's men were sailing in uncharted seas. They steered their ships north along the African coast, not knowing what to expect.

They confronted two obstacles immediately. The first was the powerful Mozambique Current, which flows from north to south along the coast of southeastern Africa. After fighting the current for four days, the Portuguese were discouraged to discover that they were exactly where they had started. Eventually, however, they began to make headway, and by December 25, they had advanced north of the Great Fish River. In honor of the nativity of Jesus Christ they gave the name Natal to the land they were passing; the region, which is today one of the four provinces of South Africa, is still known by that name.

The second obstacle the explorers faced was scurvy, a deadly disease that was the scourge of long-distance mariners. Scurvy causes the skin to turn yellow, the joints to ache, and the gums to swell and bleed; people with advanced cases become weak and listless and eventually die. It is known today that scurvy is caused by a deficiency

This map, first published in Milan, Italy, in 1508, shows Portugal's sea routes around Africa to the East. Another Italian city, Venice, suffered greatly as a result of Portugal's newfound access to the lands of spices. By the time this map was published, spices in Portugal were selling for one-fifth their cost in Venice, which had previously enjoyed a dominant position in the eastern trade.

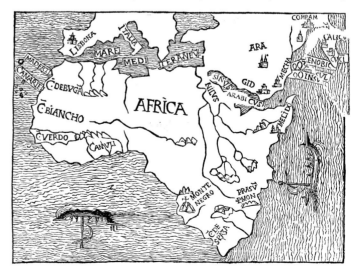

of vitamin C in the diet, but it was not until several centuries after Gama's time that sea captains learned to add
lemons, limes, onions, sauerkraut, and other sources of the
vitamin to their rations. Gama and his contemporaries
knew only that a landfall with fresh food and water often
stemmed an outbreak (the reason being that vitamin C is
plentiful in almost any fresh food), so when his men began
to suffer from sore joints and swollen gums, the captain-
major knew he had to find an anchorage.

In early January the fleet spent five days anchored off a
friendly village. The Portuguese were welcomed ashore;
they traded gifts with the natives and ferried fresh water
out to the ships in native canoes. The location of this
landing place is uncertain, but it was somewhere along
the southern coast of present-day Mozambique, at a spot
the Portuguese named Terra da Boa Gente (Land of the
Good People) for the generosity of its inhabitants, whose
chief "said we were welcome to anything in his country of
which we stood in need."

Several weeks later the fleet reached the mouth of the
Quelimane River, also in present-day Mozambique. By this
point the ships needed to be careened again, and scurvy
was ravaging the crew. Some men had died. Many others
were ill, "their feet and hands swelling, and their gums
growing over their teeth, so they could not eat"; they
needed fresh food and a long rest ashore. Gama ordered
the fleet to put in at Quelimane, where it spent more
than a month.

Though they did not realize it, the Portuguese had
reached known waters. Gama had sailed right past the
southernmost outpost of Arab influence on the east coast
of Africa, the trading center of Sofala. Not long after the
fleet landed at Quelimane, according to the *Roteiro*, it was
visited by several "gentlemen of the country" who were
"very haughty." The visitors wore the badges of Muslim
pilgrims in their headgear; one of them had traveled widely and had even seen European ships in the Mediterra-

nean. All of this indicated to the Portuguese captain-major that his fleet had entered the realm of Muslim East Africa. Before leaving Lisbon, Gama had been granted access to the secret reports given the crown by a fellow countryman who had traveled in this region, so he believed that he had some idea of what he would encounter on the next leg of his journey.

When Gama arrived in East Africa, the Muslim civilizaion of the Indian Ocean was a patchwork of small sultanates, rival city-states, and trade concessions. For centuries Arab merchants had plied the waters of the Red Sea, the Persian Gulf, and the Arabian Sea. Gradually, they had extended their voyages down the coasts of both East Africa and India, where they established trading posts and bartered with the local inhabitants for goods: ivory, gold, and slaves from Africa and gemstones, spices, and silks from India.

The Arabs also carried the Arabic language and the religion of Islam to these lands. By Gama's time the major ports of East Africa were under the control of Arab or African Muslims, and in India many of the native Hindu peoples and their rajahs, or kings, owed allegiance to Muslim sultans. Although Gama had returned to the known world, that did not mean he could abandon caution: the Muslims who monopolized this huge trading empire did not welcome the arrival of upstart Europeans in the Indian Ocean. From Quelimane, Gama intended to work his way up the coast, stopping at ports to buy provisions, until he could hire a local pilot. Through centuries of trade with Arab merchants in the Middle East, Europeans had learned that the crossing of the Indian Ocean—especially the northern arm of it, called the Arabian Sea—was a tricky business. The winds changed direction with the seasons and the arrival of the monsoons, and the route was dotted with thousands of islands, reefs, and shoals, each of them a potential shipwreck. The safest and most efficient way to reach India from the African coast was to recruit a pilot, or guide, who was familiar with the passage.

But obtaining a pilot proved irksomely difficult. Gama's first stop was the port of Moçambique, where the hazards of navigating in unknown waters were immediately demonstrated: the *Berrio* ran aground on a sandbar at the harbor's entrance and shattered its helm. But the rewards of reaching uncharted lands were evident as well. The author of the *Roteiro* wrote of Moçambique's inhabitants:

> Their language is the same as that of the Moors [Arabic]. They all wear toucas, with borders of silk embroidered in gold. They are merchants, and have transactions with white Moors, four of whose vessels were at the time in port, laden with gold, silver, cloves, pepper, ginger and silver rings, as also quantities of pearls, jewels, and rubies, all of which articles are used by the people of this country. . . . All these things, with the exception of the gold, were brought thither by these Moors; and we were told that further on, where we were going to, they abounded, and that precious stones, pearls and spices were so plentiful that there was no need to purchase them, as they could be collected in baskets.

With the help of crew members who spoke Arabic, Gama offered the local sultan a handsome amount of gold and two silk robes in exchange for the services of two pilots. The sultan agreed, but the Portuguese met armed resistance when they tried to take the second pilot. Angered by the sultan's duplicity, Gama opened fire with the bombards and seized the pilot by force. Then, when the sultan refused to supply the Portuguese with fresh water, they bombarded the town and took prisoners.

The unwilling pilots were not very helpful and had to be flogged. When the fleet anchored off Mombasa, in present-day Kenya, they managed to desert. A furious Gama ordered two of the other prisoners he had taken at Moçambique to be tortured; boiling oil was dropped on their skin until they revealed their intention to have the ships seized by the Arabs as soon as they entered the port, in revenge for the actions of the Portuguese at

An Arab dhow. The Arabs had acted as middlemen in the trade between Europe and the East for centuries. The lateen (triangular) sails used by the Arabs on their dhows inspired the Portuguese to use similar rigging on their caravels, the ships that carried so many of their mariners on their voyages of exploration.

Moçambique. The tortured men, whose hands were bound, then threw themselves into the sea and drowned. The Portuguese responded "to the malice and treachery planned by these dogs" by seizing two local boats and ordering the new prisoners to serve as pilots.

The prisoners taken at Mombasa assured Gama that at Malindi, a short distance up the coast, he would find many pilots. So the fleet made for Malindi, and there, to his relief, Gama received a warm welcome. The sultan of Malindi, an enemy of the sultan of Mombasa, was more than willing to befriend Gama; perhaps he hoped that as allies the Portuguese would offer him some advantage against his local enemies. Although Gama refused to go ashore, fearing further treachery, the sultan visited the fleet in his own boat, and the two men exchanged gifts. Gama released all his prisoners, and the sultan provided a willing and able pilot for the voyage to India.

The identity of this pilot has been much debated by historians. The author of the *Roteiro* says that he was a Christian from India, where a small colony of Christians is known to have existed since the 1st century A.D., but later passages in the *Roteiro* suggest that Gama's crewmen were not very good at determining the religion of people

The fortified Portuguese trading center at Calicut; from a 16th-century Portuguese manuscript. Gama was the first European mariner to call at Calicut, which would always be notably more resistant to Portuguese influence than Goa, another important port city farther north on the Malabar Coast.

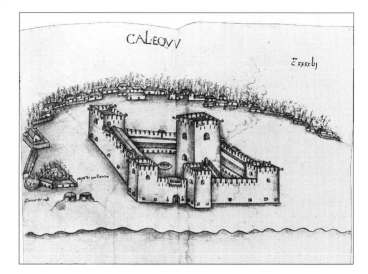

they met on the voyage: the Portuguese had a tendency to identify non-Muslims, especially Hindus, as Christians. Other sources claim that the pilot was either an Arab or an Indian Muslim, possibly even Ibn Majid, a pilot and mathematician who called himself the Lion of the Sea in Fury. The author of several volumes of sailing instructions in Arabic, Ibn Majid was the foremost Indian Ocean navigator of his day and is known to have been living in East Africa at the time of Gama's journey.

Though his identity may never be known beyond doubt, Gama's pilot knew his business, and he faithfully led the Portuguese to their destination. The three ships left Malindi on April 24, 1498, and reached the city of Calicut, on the west coast of India, on May 20. These were the first European vessels ever to reach India, and their arrival marked a turning point in world history.

The nations of Europe had been searching for a sea route to India and the East for many years. Portugal had searched longer and harder than any other country, and at last Gama had proved that it was possible to reach India by sailing around Africa. The voyage ended centuries of confusion about the shape of Africa as well. The immediate result of the voyage for Portugal was a period of unprecedented national prosperity and power. Gama's achievement was the triumphant climax of a decades-long effort that constituted one of the first systematic national programs of exploration.

But Vasco da Gama's voyage was also a beginning—the start of a new enterprise of commerce and colonization. By pioneering the passage to India and beyond, Gama opened the way for centuries of European empirebuilding in Africa and Asia. Portugal led the way south and east, and the other nations of Europe were swift to follow. When Gama's three battered wooden ships sailed into the port of Calicut, one era of exploration ended, and a new era of exploitation began.

A Land Looking Out to Sea

Portugal would seem an unlikely candidate for the role of world power. A small country, with a total land area of just 35,383 square miles, Portugal is only about the size of the state of Indiana, or less than one-fifth the size of Spain, its neighbor on the Iberian Peninsula. Portugal lies at the westernmost edge of continental Europe, surrounded by Spain to the east and north and the Atlantic Ocean to the south and west.

Although Portugal is not completely isolated from the rest of Europe, geographical barriers make travel difficult: by sea, the notoriously rough Bay of Biscay separates Portugal from France and Great Britain, and by land, low but rugged mountain ranges guard the Spanish border, beyond which is the hot, high plateau of central Spain. Spain, in turn, is separated from the rest of Europe by the Pyrenees Mountains along its border with France.

Until the late Middle Ages, religion and politics also helped isolate Portugal from the rest of Europe. In the 8th century, the entire Iberian Peninsula had been overrun by the Moors, a diverse group of Islamic North Africans. The Moors thereby controlled the western Mediterranean Sea, including the Strait of Gibraltar, the narrow seaway between Europe and Africa that gives Portugal access to the Mediterranean Sea. The Christian reconquest of the peninsula took several centuries. For his services in fighting against the Moors, a nobleman known to history as King Alfonso I was granted recognition by a grateful papacy

An example of Moorish architecture in Spain. The Moors ruled much of the Iberian Peninsula, including the regions that would become the nation of Portugal, from the 8th through the 15th centuries.

as the rightful monarch of the independent kingdom of Portugal in 1179.

Throughout the long period of conquest, reconquest, and nationbuilding, few travelers from elsewhere in Europe visited Portugal, and the country sent few emissaries abroad. Not long after it had freed itself from the domination of the Moors and established its independence, Portugal, like much of the rest of Europe, was devastated by the Black Death, a series of epidemics of bubonic and pneumonic plague that killed at least half the population of the continent. At the beginning of the 15th century, as it was beginning to recover from the worst outbreak of the plague, Portugal's population stood at no more than 1 million people. Yet within a century, this small, isolated nation of relatively few citizens, largely bereft of natural resources, was to become the most powerful nation on earth.

This incredibly detailed engraving of the city of Lisbon appeared in the Universal Cosmography *(first published in 1575) of André Thevet, a seagoing French monk who made several trips to the New World. Like the holy city of Rome, the oldest sections of Lisbon are built on seven hills.*

Portugal rose to power on the waves of the sea. As Great Britain and the Netherlands were to reaffirm in later centuries, the ocean offered a world of opportunity to small nations. With a 500-mile coastline on the Atlantic, Portugal turned its back on the mountains and highlands of its landward borders and cast its destiny with the sea.

Two industries developed side by side: fishing and ship-building. Portugal's fishing fleet became one of Europe's largest, its boatmen and sailors highly skilled. Like virtually all mariners of the day, Portugal's fishermen stayed fairly close to shore, navigating by studying landmarks along the coasts and rarely venturing far out of sight of land. Their maps were the *portolani*, or pilot charts, that gave sailing instructions from port to port and were widely circulated among sailors, but more often they trusted to their own ability to read the ever-shifting patterns of wind, current, and tide. They were keen observers of the weather, and they could decode information from such clues as the flight of a bird or the sight of a floating weed.

Shipbuilding flourished in Portugal after the Moors were driven out. The complicated history of Portuguese ship-building—made more difficult because the same word was often used at different times or in various places to describe two very different types of ship—has not yet been fully unraveled by scholars, but it is certain that Portuguese ships had two ancestors: the square-sailed, deep-hulled cargo galley that had been used in the Mediterranean for thousands of years, and the Arab vessel, developed in the Arabian Sea trade, that is generally called the *dhow* and has a curved or triangular sail, known as a lateen sail. During the late Middle Ages, Portuguese ships evolved from these ancestors into several categories.

The *barca* and the *varinel* were used for coastal fishing and the river trade; neither was suitable for the open sea. The *barca* was small, with square sails; the *varinel* was a version of the Mediterranean galley that was powered by a com-bination of sails and oars. The *nau* was a larger, cargo-car-

A 15th-century illustration of Portuguese ships, which were generally much smaller and more maneuverable than the huge cargo vessels used in the Mediterranean at the time.

rying ship with two masts for square sails; some later versions added a third mast for a lateen sail. All of these ships were in use by the early 14th century, when King Dinis created Portugal's first navy and ordered the planting of royal pine forests specifically to provide timber for the future construction of ships.

By that time, Europe was begining to awaken from what the historian Daniel J. Boorstin has termed the "Great Interruption" of geographical knowledge, and curious and learned Europeans were beginning to piece together bits of geographical knowledge into a new picture of the world. Although it is far from true, as is often stated, that before Christopher Columbus's 1492 voyage all Europeans believed the world to be flat, that oft-quoted generalization does correctly suggest that medieval Europe's geographical conceptions owed more to superstition and legend than to empirical knowledge.

The ancient Greeks and Romans had understood that the world is round; in the 3rd century B.C., a Greek mathematician named Eratosthenes had even made a highly accurate estimate of the distance around it. But after the fall of the Roman Empire in the 5th century A.D., the study of geography faltered in Europe. At the same time, it was flourishing in the Muslim world, encouraged by the Arab mariners and merchants who sailed the Arabian Sea and by the learned Arab scholars who traveled throughout the Islamic Empire. While the Arabs were preserving the scientific works of the Greeks and Romans and adding to them studies of their own, Europe's geographic curiosity was being stifled by a Christian viewpoint that held the Bible to be the repository of all necessary knowledge about the world. In medieval Europe, curiosity about geography and other sciences came to be regarded as a form of vanity, and certain knowledge as heresy. According to this worldview, the earth was flat, with Jerusalem at its center. Places mentioned in the Bible, such as the Garden of Eden, were often drawn on maps; even Columbus, who did so much to revolutionize humankind's concept of the world, believed that on his third voyage he had discovered the earthly paradise.

This static view of the world began to change in the 11th and 12th centuries. Through contact with the Moors, Europeans were exposed to the scholarship of medieval Arab civilization, including copies of the works of Eratosthenes and other ancient writers. From these sources, educated Europeans gradually became familiar with such ideas as a round earth.

One geographer who was reintroduced to Europe by the Arabs was Claudius Ptolemaeus, called Ptolemy, who wrote a *Guide to Geography* in the 2nd century A.D. Arab scholars discovered Ptolemy's *Geography* in the 9th century, and in 1410 it appeared in a Latin translation, available to European readers for the first time in many centuries. Ptolemy's ideas about the world were widely adopted in Europe.

This 8th-century map of the world illustrates some of the fanciful notions of geography then prevalent in Europe.

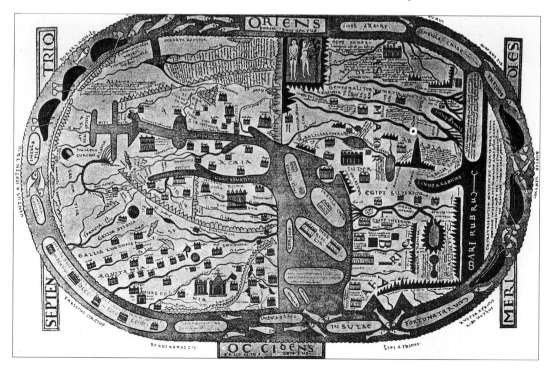

Ptolemy was the father of modern cartography, or map-making. He originated the system of grids—lines of latitude and longitude—that makes accurate mapping possible. Yet, as Boorstin points out, "while Ptolemy's *theory* of map-making could not be faulted, the maps that had become attached to his *Geography* contained some crucial errors which would shape the future of world exploration."

Many aspects of the Ptolemaic worldview were fanciful or just plain wrong. Ptolemy believed that somewhere far to the south there must be a large landmass to "balance" the mass of Europe and Asia; this hypothetical continent was called the Terra Incognita, or Unknown Land. He also believed that both Africa and China were joined to the Terra Incognita in the south, making the Indian Ocean a closed inland sea. Some 15th-century mapmakers disagreed with Ptolemy: on a map produced in 1459 by a Venetian monk named Fra Mauro, Africa is a huge peninsula and the Indian Ocean is part of the open sea. As Gama's voyage would eventually prove, Mauro's view was correct.

Beginning in about the 11th century, while Europe was being exposed to the works of the classical and Arab geographers, Europeans began traveling to the Holy Land—the present-day countries of Israel, Lebanon, and Syria—either as religious pilgrims or as crusaders to reclaim the region from the Muslims who controlled it. These travelers from the West found spices, silks, and other exotic goods in the ports and markets of the Middle East. Luxury items such as these aroused great excitement and fetched great prices throughout Europe, and Europeans began to exhibit a fresh curiosity about the source of these imported goods, most of which originated in lands that lay beyond the boundaries of the so-called known world. This curiosity was whetted by the fabulous tales spun by travelers such as the Venetian merchant-adventurer Marco Polo, who journeyed to China in the 13th century.

The long land route from the Middle East across Asia had been used by trade caravans for many centuries, but only

comptrvons autres dples.

Du plam pam de formose er de la valer doubteuse

The Venetian traveler Marco Polo arrives at a walled port city in the course of his fabulous journey. The illustration is from an early-15th-century French manuscript entitled The Book of Wonders, *which contains Polo's narrative of his adventures as well as the accounts of other explorer's travels. Polo's narrative,* A Description of the World, *did much to dispel preposterous European notions about world geography and stimulated intense interest in the Far East.*

in the 13th century, when all of Asia was unified under strong Mongol rulers like Khublai Khan, was it possible for a European like Polo to travel the length of it and back again. As the Mongol Empire began to break up, warring states arose throughout Asia, and the land route became too hazardous to traverse. By the 14th century, the Muslim civilizations of the Middle East and the Arabian Sea controlled all trade with Asia.

This commerce involved many types of goods, but spices were the most highly prized in Europe. Within a few years of their introduction, pepper, nutmeg, cinnamon, and cloves were in wide use. They helped preserve the food of the Middle Ages, and they added great variety to its often dreary taste. Various imported herbs, roots, leaves, seeds, aromatic resins, and other substances—all also classified as spices—were used as perfumes, as medicines, and in religious rituals. Europeans could not get enough spices, and they were a source of great wealth for the merchants and states that controlled the trade in them.

The European end of the spice trade was largely controlled by powerful banking and merchant families in the Italian city-states of Genoa and Venice. The Italian dealers bought the spices at Arab market centers—Alexandria, in Egypt, and Antioch, in Syria, were two of the most important—where they had been brought, for the most part, by ship or camel caravan from India's west, or Malabar, coast. Some of the spices, such as certain types of pepper, originated in India, but most came from places farther east: the islands strung across the vast sweep of tropical sea between India and New Guinea. Today, most of these islands are part of the nations of Malaysia and Indonesia; in the 14th century Europeans called them the Spice Islands.

The Spice Islands were part of what Europeans called the Indies. The precise meaning of this term varied; it could refer to the Spice Islands or, more specifically, to a small cluster of spice-rich Indonesian islands called the Moluccas. It could be used in a broader sense to include all the islands east of India, or India itself. Occasionally, its meaning encompassed part of East Africa, particularly the remote mountain kingdom of Abyssinia (present-day Ethiopia). China, which was called Cathay by Europeans of the late Middle Ages, was also sometimes considered to be part of the Indies. The vagueness of the term can be attributed to the limited knowledge of the geography of the Far East held by even the most educated Europeans at the time. They knew—by rumor more than by experience—that these places existed, but they were not sure exactly where they were located.

Tucked away at the westernmost edge of Europe, without a Mediterranean port, Portugal played no role in the spice trade that flourished between the Italians and the Arabs at the eastern end of the Mediterranean. Instead, by the mid-14th century the Portuguese were making their first tentative forays in the opposite direction, into the Atlantic Ocean and toward the offshore islands.

There are four island groups in the Atlantic Ocean off the coast of Portugal and North Africa. The northernmost and westernmost is the Azores. South of the Azores, and much closer to the mainland, is the Madeira group; its principal islands are Madeira and Porto Santo. South of

During his 48-year reign, which lasted from 1385 to 1433, King João I, known as the Great, secured Portugal's independence from Spain and initiated his nation's age of exploration, conquest, and colonization with his attack on the Moorish stronghold of Ceuta in 1415.

Madeira, and closest to the mainland, are the Canary Islands. The southernmost group, a bit farther from land than the Canaries, are the Cape Verde Islands. At least one of these island clusters, probably the Canaries, was known to the mariners of the ancient world, although its location was later forgotten. By the 14th century, the Canaries—and probably the Azores and the Madeiras—had again been sighted by European seamen.

In 1341, King Afonso IV of Portugal sent a fleet of three ships south to investigate the rumors of islands in the sea. The ships reached the Canary Islands and captured four of the Guanches, the native inhabitants of the Canaries. Upon their return to Portugal, the captains reported that the islands contained dyewood, a tree that was prized because its bark yielded a useful dye. Portugal made no attempt to colonize the Canaries, but before many years had passed, colonists from both Spain and France had settled there. Spain eventually won possession, and the Canary Islands remain Spanish territory.

A new era in Portuguese history began in 1385, when a nobleman named João took the Portuguese throne and established a new dynasty, the House of Avis. One of his first acts was to make an alliance with Britain; to seal the accord he married an English noblewoman, Philippa of Lancaster, who bore him six children. The third, born in 1394, was a son who was named Henrique, or Henry. According to Gomes Eanes de Zurara, the first chronicler of Portugal's glorious seafaring age, it was foretold in the stars at Henry's birth that "this prince was bound to engage in great and noble conquests, and above all was he bound to attempt the discovery of things which were hidden from other men, and secret." In fulfilling this destiny, Prince Henry, known to modern historians as the Navigator, launched the great era of European maritime exploration.

PRINCE HENRY
OF
PORTUGALL

HONI · SOIT · QVI · MAL · Y · PENSE

CEVTA

Prince Henry and the Navigators

Little is known about Prince Henry's youth. The royal family maintained residences in both Oporto, the coastal city in northern Portugal where Henry was born, and Lisbon, farther south, on the north bank of the estuary of the Tagus River, which steadily grew in importance and became Portugal's leading city.

With his older brothers Duarte and Pedro, Henry studied the subjects that constituted the education of a medieval prince: the strategies and tactics of warfare, the arts of diplomacy and statecraft, and ancient and modern history. King João admired learning; his court had an intellectual flavor and a large and well-stocked library. Both Duarte and Pedro read widely and later wrote books of their own. It is likely that Henry's reading was equally extensive, although it is not known whether he ever wrote anything; no works by him have survived.

Although by Henry's day the Moors had long since been driven from Portugal, they still occupied parts of Spain and all of North Africa. Around 1410, King João decided to attack the Moorish stronghold of Ceuta, in present-day Morocco on the Strait of Gibraltar. To the pope and the Christian nations of Europe—and to Henry, who was exceptionally pious—fighting Muslims was a worthy and holy endeavor, but João had economic incentives as well: Ceuta was an important trade hub where Mediterranean cargo ships and camel caravans called regularly, and the Portuguese wanted to muscle into this profitable commerce.

This facsimile of a rare Dutch engraving shows Prince Henry the Navigator on a bluff outside Ceuta as his forces lay siege to the city. Like the crusade against Ceuta, many of Henry's actions were inspired by his intense religious beliefs; he was a devout ascetic who practiced lifelong celibacy and often wore a hair shirt beneath his princely finery.

The Rock of Gibraltar was the western gateway to the Mediterranean Sea, which was medieval Europe's most important commercial artery. Portugal's location as the westernmost nation on the Continent prevented it from playing an active role in the Mediterranean trade and necessitated that its mariners take to the oceans.

Preparation for the invasion of Ceuta took several years. When Henry was about 19 years of age, his father sent him to Oporto to assemble the fleet that would carry the Portuguese across the strait. The prince excelled as marshal of the fleet, and when the Portuguese invaded Ceuta in 1415, he valorously led the assault. The city fell in a day, costing the invaders only eight dead, but Henry's ideals about the motives of his men suffered a casualty. "Don't imagine that your men are still interested in fighting the Moors," he was told by a more experienced campaigner as the city's defenses were being overrun. "They're all over the town plundering the empty houses."

The spoils of war were lavish indeed. When the Moors abandoned Ceuta to the Portuguese, they left behind silks, beautifully woven rugs, spices, ivory, salt, gold, silver, and gems. This wealth had been garnered by trade with Asia and inner Africa, and the Portuguese were dazzled with visions of riches from the far places of the world.

João's court and fleet soon returned to Lisbon, leaving a small force in charge of Ceuta. Three years later, Ceuta was besieged by a Moorish army, and Henry led the relief force, then spent three months in Ceuta—three months that changed the history of the world.

While in Ceuta, Henry learned a great deal about the geography and commerce of northern Africa. He talked to prisoners and merchants about the caravans that came out of the bleak, mountain-rimmed desert south of the city, and he learned of ancient and well-used routes that led across the desert, 20 days' travel, to a "Green Country" in the south. From this forested and fertile region—present-day Guinea, Gambia, Senegal, and southern Mali and Niger—caravans brought salt, African pepper, gold, and "elephant's teeth" (ivory). He learned that the Muslim traders practiced a "silent trade" with the African peoples south of the desert: a Muslim trader set out a pile of goods, such as salt from the desert, cloth, coral beads, or brass utensils. The Africans then came forward and set out a corresponding amount of gold or ivory. Each party then added or subtracted goods until a bargain was struck. The chronicler Zurara says these tales fired Henry's imagination and made him determined to reach the Green Country, which the Europeans called Guinea. But he would seek Guinea not across the desert, with which the Portuguese had no experience, but by sea.

Henry returned to Portugal in 1419. He planned an attack on the Moorish citadel of Gibraltar, but King João forbade the venture as strategically unwise. Some historians have suggested that it was Henry's irritation at having his plans thwarted that made him abandon the royal court at Lisbon in favor of settlement in the remote Algarve, Portugal's southernmost province, where he was made governor and took up residence on Cape St. Vincent, a high, windswept headland jutting out into the Atlantic. He built a fort and residence in a village called Sagres, which became the jumping-off point for a decades-long series of ventures into the unknown.

The prince invited sailors, sea captains, geographers, mapmakers, and travelers and scholars of all sorts to visit him at Sagres to share their knowledge and ideas. He assembled a library of books about travel, including a

Prince Henry and his navigators look out to sea from the royal observatory at Sagres. There, Henry brought together astronomers, cartographers, shipbuilders, and mariners of many different nationalities and faiths—Jews, Muslims, Arabs, Italians, Germans, and Scandinavians as well as Portuguese—in order to make a comprehensive study of the science of exploration.

Caravels in full sail among a school of flying fish. The first caravels designed by Henry and his men at Sagres were small, just big enough to carry the supplies and provisions needed by those who manned them, because the most valuable cargo they brought back to the Navigator was information about the new lands his mariners explored in them.

manuscript of Marco Polo's *Description of the World* brought from Italy by Henry's brother Pedro and several copies of Ptolemy's *Geography*. Henry also obtained copies of many maps, and he had new ones made. He sponsored mathematicians and craftsmen who produced new navigational instruments, such as improved compasses, the quadrant (a device for measuring altitude, or height above sea level), and the cross-staff (a simplified version of the astrolabe, which is used to measure latitude, the distance north or south of the equator).

As ships are obviously essential to maritime navigation and exploration, Henry and his advisers devoted a great

deal of their energies to shipbuilding. Governmental po-
licies that encouraged the craft were already in place:
anyone constructing a ship of more than 100 tons was
entitled to free timber from the royal forest, and any
necessary other materials could be imported tax-free. At
the port town of Lagos, not far from Sagres, shipwrights
collaborated with sea captains to design and build vessels
specifically suited for the kind of open-sea sailing in which
Henry was interested. By about 1440, they had created the
caravel, which was similar to the little craft used on the
rivers of northern Portugal. Although caravels had some
cargo space, they were much smaller than the massive trade
ships of the Mediterranean. They were nimble and rode
high in the water, making them easy to maneuver and able
to sail close to unknown shores, where rocks and sandbars
might tear the hull out of a heavier vessel, and they were
equipped with lateen sails, like the Arab dhow. Lateen sails
enabled a caravel to sail against the wind much more easily
than a square-rigged ship, making its captain much less
dependent upon the direction of the prevailing breezes.
Caravels therefore made faster and surer trips than square-
riggers, and they played a key role in the opening of the
world. "The best ships that sailed the seas" was how Alvise
Cadamosto, one of Henry's navigators, described them;
Columbus's famous *Niña*, *Pinta*, and *Santa María* were of
caravel design.

Henry sent his first ship—a square-rigged barca captained
by João Gonçalves Zarco and Tristão Vaz Teixeira, two
young squires of his household—south in search of Guinea
in 1419 or 1420. After being blown off course to westward
and landing in the Madeiras on an island that they named
Porto Santo, Zarco and Teixeira returned to Sagres. Henry
questioned them carefully about their experience, then
decided to claim and colonize the Madeiras. A colonizing
expedition was dispatched to the islands in 1420.

In the years that followed, Henry sent his ships out in two
directions. Some went west and southwest to discover and

(continued on page 44)

The Consequences of Colonization

~~~~~~~~~

During the age of exploration and expansion that began with Prince Henry, Europeans moved into many parts of the world, some inhabited, some not. Deliberately or accidentally, the newcomers nearly always changed the lands they found. Modern historians and environmentalists point to the Portuguese colonization of the Madeira Islands as one of the earliest examples of how the arrival of outsiders can change an isolated, self-contained ecosystem.

One change was a biological intrusion. Bartolomeu Perestrello, leader of the expedition sent by Henry to colonize the islands in 1420, took with him a rabbit who happened to be pregnant. She and her offspring were released on the island of Porto Santo—a rabbit's paradise, for there was plenty of vegetation and no predators and no diseases. As is their wont, the rabbits multiplied quickly and devoured everything, including the crops planted by the settlers. Things got so bad that the settlers actually had to flee from rabbit-infested Porto Santo to Madeira Island.

But Madeira Island itself was being changed as its native ecosystem was destroyed. To clear land for farming, the settlers set fires to burn off brush and forest, which they were then unable to control. The fires burned for seven years and left the island largely deforested and covered with a thick layer of ash. Later, grapevines from Crete were planted to replace the forests, and the vines flourished in the ash-rich soil, producing grapes that could be made into fine wines—especially the strong golden wines that are still called Madeiras.

A third change was deliberate. Prince Henry ordered sugarcane from Sicily planted on Porto Santo and Madeira. At the time, sugar was a great luxury in Europe, and only the wealthy could afford it. The imported cane plants throve in the Madeiras, setting off a series of chain reactions with far-reaching consequences.

Sugar from the Madeiras increased the supply of the sweetener in the marketplaces of Europe, driving the price down, which meant that more people could afford it. As more people were exposed to the taste of sugar, the demand for it increased correspondingly. As a result, the first Spanish settlers in the Americas—on islands such as Hispaniola, Jamaica, and Cuba—planted sugarcane and enslaved first the Native Americans of the Caribbean and then blacks imported from Africa to tend the crop. In a sense, Prince Henry's successful economic experiment in the Madeiras contributed to the growth of the transatlantic slave trade.

But the Portuguese were concerned primarily that the Madeira Islands yield a profit. The pattern for their future endeavors was set. Exploration might be carried out for all sorts of lofty motives—the drive to expand the realm of human knowledge, the desire to spread Christianity, the patriotic urge to plant one's flag on distant shores—but in the end, exploration would be expected to pay its way.

Albrecht Dürer's drawing of a hare. The greatest German artist of the Renaissance, Dürer was fascinated by the discoveries made by the mariners of the Iberian Peninsula.

(continued from page 41)

A medieval German astrolabe, an instrument used in the Middle Ages to fix latitude by measuring the position of heavenly bodies. Astrolabes were extremely difficult to use, especially at sea; at Sagres, Henry and his men devised the simpler cross-staff, which enabled mariners to fix their position north or south of the equator by measuring the angle of the sun's elevation above the horizon at noon.

colonize the Atlantic islands, and others went south, working their way down the bulging coast of northern Africa. The two ventures were closely related. Stocked by Henry's colonists with sheep and cattle, the islands became regular stopping points for his coastal voyagers, supply stations where a captain could be assured of finding meat and other provisions, fresh water, wood, and safe harbors. But although he urged his mariners ever southward along the coast, there is no evidence that Henry had in mind the discovery of a route around Africa to the Indies. According to Zurara, his objectives were quite different: "To discover what lay beyond the Canaries and Cape Bojador; to trade with any Christians who might dwell in the lands beyond; to discover the extent of the Mohammedan [Islamic] dominions; to find a Christian king who would help him fight the infidel; to spread the Christian faith . . . to find Guinea."

After the settlement of the Madeiras, the next step in Henry's island venture was an attempt upon the Canary Islands. The archipelago was claimed by France and Spain, although only a handful of men from either nation had set foot on the islands. Around 1424, Henry sent a large fleet to the Canaries, but his soldiers were defeated by the Guanches and the rugged terrain. Further attempts, all unsuccessful, were made in 1427, 1435, 1440, and 1445. The Portuguese finally won a foothold on one island but the captain Henry sent to govern was driven out by the Guanches. By the end of the 15th century, Portugal had relinquished its claims in the Canaries to Spain.

Henry had better luck with the other island groups. In the late 1420s his navigator Gonçalo Velho Cabral discovered and explored the Azores, and in 1432 Henry sent 16 ships, hundreds of men, a priest, and dozens of farm animals to populate these islands, which are almost one-third of the way across the Atlantic Ocean from Portugal. The Cape Verde Islands were discovered much later, as a fortuitous consequence of the coastal exploration of Africa. In 1456, Alvise Cadamosto, a Venetian sailing in Henry's service along the African coast, was blown out to sea and landed in the Cape Verdes. Diogo Gomes, a Portuguese captain, also claimed to have discovered the Cape Verdes at about the same time; within a few years, the islands belonged to the Portuguese crown. Like the Madeiras and the Azores, they became useful supply bases.

When King João died in 1433, he was succeeded by Duarte, Henry's oldest brother. By this time, Henry had established his claim to the Madeiras and the Azores and been turned away from the Canaries; he could now focus his attention on his southward venture—the exploration of the African coast. The first obstacle his mariners had to overcome was Cape Bojador, on the African mainland just south of the Canary Islands.

Cape Bojador was the southern limit of knowledge. In Europe's historical memory, no mariner had sailed beyond it. Beyond it lay what Arab geographers fearfully called the Green Sea of Darkness, a mysterious region of eternal fog and bewildering currents, and, farther south, the Torrid Zone, where, it was said, the sea boiled and the burning sun turned men's flesh black. Between 1422 and 1434, Henry commissioned at least 14 separate voyages to round the Cape; all returned unsuccessful. According to Zurara,

> to say the truth this was not from cowardice or want of good will, but from the novelty of the thing and the wide-spread and ancient rumor about this Cape, that had been cherished by the mariners from generation to generation. . . . For certainly it cannot be presumed that among so many noble men who did such great and lofty deeds for the glory of their memory, there had not been one to dare this deed. But being satisfied of the peril, and seeing no hope of honor or profit, they left off the attempt. For, said the mariners, this much is clear, that beyond this Cape there is no race

of men nor place of inhabitants . . . while the currents
are so terrible that no ship having once passed the
Cape, will ever be able to return. . . . These mariners
of ours . . . [were] threatened not only by fear but by
its shadow.

Finally, in 1434, Gil Eanes, a squire from Sagres, making
his second try at the dreaded Cape, succeeded in passing
Bojador. He landed on a sandy beach and returned quite
uncharred to Lagos, boasting that the Green Sea of Darkness was "as easy to sail in as the waters at home." The
specter of Bojador had been laid to rest. "Although the
matter was a small one in itself," wrote Zurara, "yet on
account of its daring it was reckoned great."

Henry sent Eanes out again the next year, accompanied
by Afonso Baldaia, another young squire. Some 100 miles
past Bojador they found the footprints of men and camels
on a deserted beach—signs of life in an empty landscape.
A year after that, on a separate voyage, Baldaia reached a
point far south of Cape Bojador and brought back a valuable cargo of sealskins. Despite these achievements and
Henry's ever-mounting curiosity, the prince had to call a
halt to his explorations for six years, for Portugal was
planning an invasion of the Moorish stronghold of Tangier,
and Henry was to serve as one of the commanders. The
invasion proved a disaster—among the Portuguese casualties was Henry's younger brother, Prince Fernando, who
died in a Moorish dungeon after being taken prisoner—
King Duarte died the following year, and the dynastic
quarrels that ensued kept Henry at court in Lisbon until
1441, when he was at last able to return to Sagres and
resume Portugal's exploration of the African coast.

In some ways, Henry now had a freer hand, for Duarte had
been critical of many of his enterprises, considering them
too hastily conceived and the expenditures involved too
lavish, with no prospect of immediate economic return.
The same year that Henry resumed his efforts, Antão
Gonçalves returned to the place that Baldaia had visited

and brought back a dozen slaves. Their arrival marks the beginning of Europe's involvement in commerce in African slaves, although the slave trade already flourished in many parts of Africa itself. Recognizing an opportunity to silence the continuing criticism that his voyages constituted an unprofitable, frivolous quest after the unknowable, Henry immediately organized an expedition for the express purpose of taking slaves. Commanded by Gil Eanes, it set out in 1444 and brought back 235 slaves, taken by force from the Western Sahara coast—the first of millions of black Africans who would be carried away in European ships in the centuries to come.

These first slaves were sold in a field outside Lagos, and Zurara paints a vivid picture of the strange, sad scene: "What heart could be so hard as not to be pierced with piteous feeling to see that company?" he asks. "For some kept their heads low and their faces bathed in tears . . . and

Despite the advances pioneered by Henry at Sagres, open-sea navigation remained an imprecise science for centuries, and the most successful maritime explorers of the age— Gama, Columbus, Magellan— always relied on their own instincts, honed through years of experience and careful observation, as much as on scientific instruments. To laymen, the mysteries of maritime navigation, with its emphasis on celestial readings, often suggested that its practitioners were somehow akin to wizards.

it was needful to part father from son, husbands from wives, brothers from brothers . . . each fell where his lot took him. . . . Mothers would clasp their infants in their arms, and throw themselves on the ground to cover them with their bodies, disregarding an injury to their own persons, so that they could prevent their children from being separated from them." Nearby, mounted on his horse, Henry viewed the scene with the satisfaction of a zealous Christian bringing enlightenment to the heathens; Zurara remarks that the prince "reflected with great satisfaction upon the salvation of souls that before were lost." The advent of the slave trade quieted the growing public outcry about Henry's expeditions of exploration. "Then those who had been foremost in complaint grew quiet, and with soft voices praised what they had so loudly and publicly decried . . . and so they were forced to turn their blame into public praise," wrote Zurara.

The year 1441 was noteworthy for more than the birth of the European slave trade. That year, Nuno Tristão, another of Henry's navigators, made the first documented voyage in a caravel. The ship performed beautifully, and Tristão reached a new farthest-south: Cape Blanco, in present-day Mauretania. In 1444, the year of the slave raid, Tristão sailed south again and made a welcome discovery beyond Cape Blanco. Near the mouth of the Senegal River, the bleak, dry, brown coast of the Sahara gave way to a verdant, palm-fringed coastline. At last, after dozens of voyages, the Portuguese had reached the fabled Green Country.

Another milestone was reached that same year by Dinís Dias, who took a caravel south to explore the green land. Dias made for a tree-clad cape that he sighted far in the distance. When he had rounded this headland, which he called Cape Verde, he saw with delight that the coast did not simply stretch away endlessly to the south, as it did beyond Capes Bojador and Blanco, but instead fell away to the southeast. He had passed the western edge of Africa—perhaps he was close to its southern edge as well.

(continued on page 57)

Images of the World

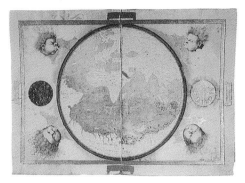

A 1519 Portuguese "mappamundi, that is to say, image of the world and of the regions which are on the earth and of the various kinds of people who inhabit it," as such documents were first described by Abraham Cresque, creator of the so-called Catalan Atlas, one of the oldest surviving world maps.

Geography is a representation in picture of the whole known world together with the phenomena which are contained therein. . . . In Geography one must contemplate the extent of the entire earth, as well as its shape . . . in order that one may rightly state what are the peculiarities and proportions of the part with which one is dealing." So wrote Ptolemy, the 2nd-century Greco-Egyptian mathematician and astronomer, in his treatise *Geography*; it was Ptolemy who established the convention of orienting a flat map with north at the top, popularized the use of a grid system of latitude and longitude for fixing location, and devised one of the first scientifically viable methods of projecting the spherical surface of the earth onto the flat surface of a map. During the Great Interruption of geographical knowledge in Europe, his work was forgotten or ignored, but during the first great age of European maritime exploration—inaugurated by Henry the Navigator from his observatory at Sagres—his reputation was revived. Those cartographers who strove to depict geographic and scientific truths about the world, rather than to illustrate Christian dogma, took Ptolemy as their guiding light, and the publishers of maps affixed his name to their products in the same way latter-day American lexicographers attached the surname Webster to their dictionaries—as an imprimatur of accuracy and authenticity. The work of some of those mapmakers who during the great age of maritime exploration strove to emulate Ptolemy in "contemplat[ing] the extent of the entire earth . . . and its position under the heavens" may be seen on this page and those that follow.

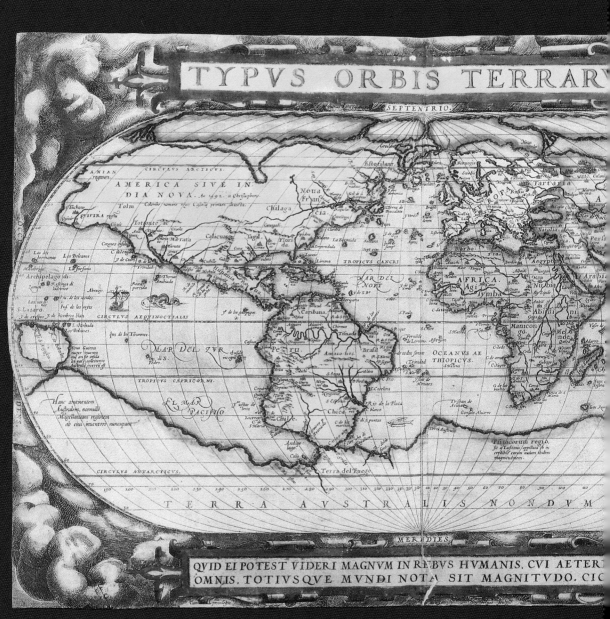

This 1579 world map appeared in that year's edition of Theatrum Orbis
Terrarum (The Picture of the World) published by the Antwerp cartographer
Abraham Ortelius, who traveled Europe collecting the best maps and the most
up-to-date information on developments in exploration. Ortelius's work (28
editions, translated into most of the languages of Europe, appeared between
1570 and his death in 1598) was the first modern geographical atlas.

The increased interest in maritime exploration in Europe was accompanied by a corresponding rise in interest in the stars, which were used by oceangoing explorers for navigational purposes. Seen here is a 1540 woodcut of a device for celestial measurements.

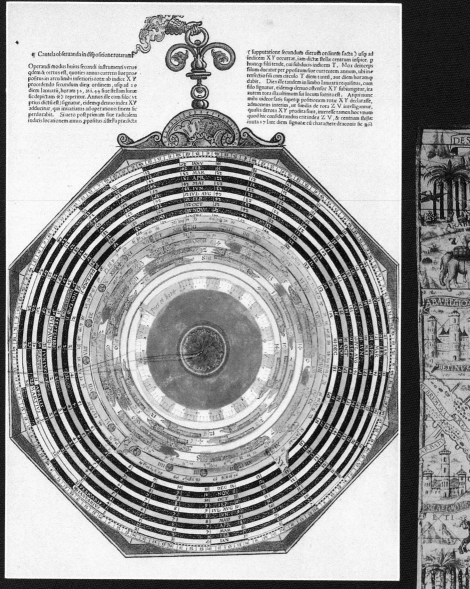

A 1540 illustration of a celestial calendar. "In Geography one must contemplate the extent of the entire earth . . . and its position under the heavens, in order that one may rightly state . . . under what parallel of the celestial sphere it is located," wrote Ptolemy.

This detail of a 1519 Portuguese world map beautifully illustrates the cartographer's adherence to Ptolemy's dictum that geography is the "representation in picture" not only of the known world but of "the phenomena contained therein."

A 1538 world map by the Flemish cartographer Gerardus Mercator, who according to the historian Daniel Boorstin "was the most original and the most influential" of Ptolemy's disciples. Mercator developed the most commonly used method of projecting the spherical earth on a flat surface, as a rectangle divided into a grid by parallel lines of longitude and latitude. Interestingly, this Mercator map ignores the discoveries of the Portuguese mariners in that, in the fashion of Ptolemy, it still depicts the Indian Ocean as a closed sea inaccessible by Dias's and Gama's routes around the southern tip of Africa.

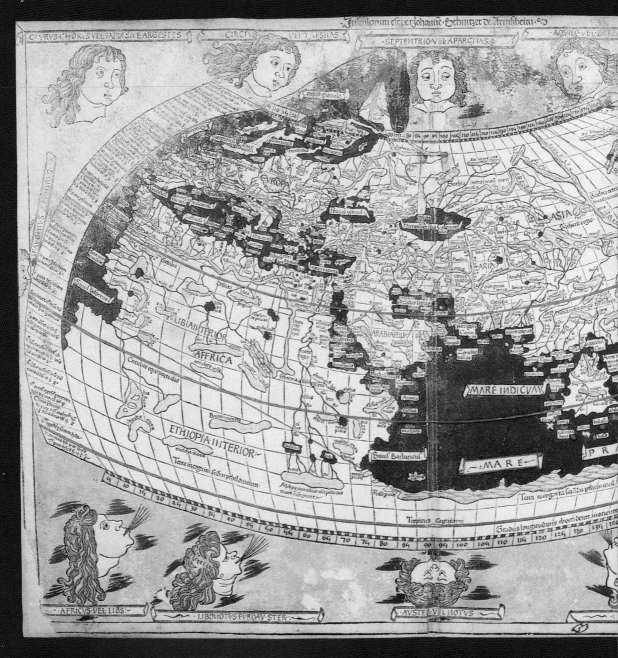

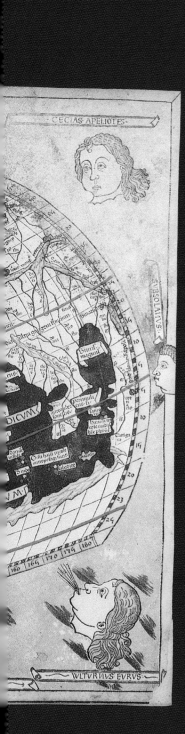

A 1540 woodcut of a celestial compass, with many of the constellations depicted figuratively.

The great age of maritime exploration ushered in by Henry the Navigator and the sea-faring men of Portugal made mapmaking big business in Europe, where ships' captains, merchants, politicians, and heads of state created a constant demand for the most recent and accurate charts and information. The best maps and atlases were constantly being revised, translated, and published in new editions in countries other than those where they originated; seen here is the title page of the first English edition, dated 1588, of The Mariners Mirrour, a Dutch compilation of charts and maps of the harbors and coastlines from Scandinavia to Morocco.

(continued from page 48)

During the mid-1440s, a number of voyages were made to the Saharan coast for slave raiding and commerce with local chieftains, who sold the Portuguese slaves and gold in exchange for cloth, mirrors, and beads. Wherever

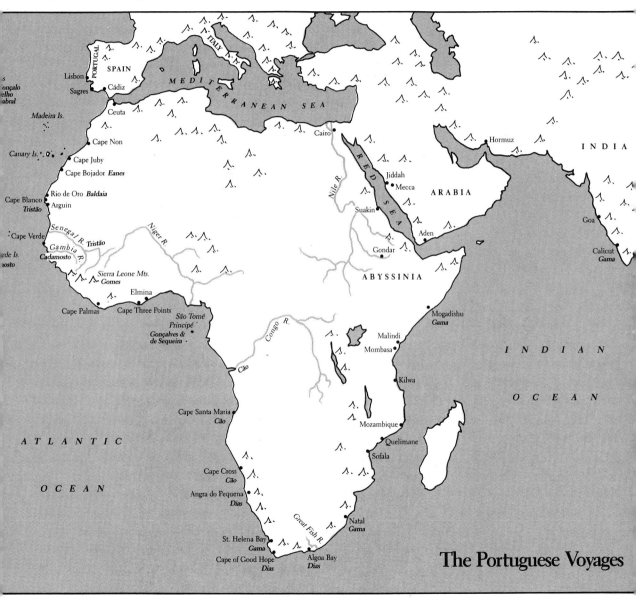

The Portuguese Voyages

the explorers went, the traders were not far behind; some captains were both explorer and trader, often during the same voyage. Soon, 25 Portuguese trade caravels were visiting the African coast each year.

In 1445, Antão Gonçalves returned to the coast to pick up João Fernandes, a sailor who at his own request had been left ashore at Arguin Bay, some 50 miles south of Cape Blanco, to study the region and find out what trade possibilities it might hold. Fernandes had met the nomadic tribespeople of the desert and traveled with them on their seasonal migrations, studying their customs as well as the wildlife, weather, and economy of the Western Sahara. Remarkably, Gonçalves managed to find him and take him back to Portugal, where his account of life in the desert fascinated Henry.

Nuno Tristão made his third and final voyage in 1446. After he passed the mouth of the Gambia River, his luck ran out. Upon reaching another river, he took two small boats and several dozen men upstream. At a native village, they were ambushed by a fleet of a dozen canoes carrying African warriors firing poisoned arrows. Tristão and most of the others were killed, and his caravel was sailed safely home by five cabin boys.

At about this time, Henry's attention was drawn away from coastal exploration by new turmoil at the royal court, where various members of the extensive royal family were trying to gain influence over young Afonso, the boy king who had succeeded his father, Duarte, on Portugal's throne. Henry also renewed his attempts to gain control of the Canary Islands, but although he was briefly successful, his control there was never firmly established. By the mid-1450s, he was again looking south.

Henry's next important navigator was not Portuguese but Venetian. When Alvise Cadamosto was exiled from his home city because of trouble with the law, he came to Sagres, met Henry, and persuaded the prince to let him enter the "Guinea trade." Cadamosto possessed an inquiring and observant mind. In 1455, he landed near Cape Blanco and made a detailed study of the land and people; among other things, he saw hippopotamuses, which he called "horse-fishes." His observations were later published as a book, one of the first exploration narratives concerning Africa to reach European readers.

On Cadamosto's second voyage, in 1456, he landed in the Cape Verde Islands. Diogo Gomes, a Portuguese navigator who sailed at the same time, also claimed to have discovered the Cape Verdes; Gomes also made a foray up the Gambia River and gathered much information about the caravan routes along which the kings of the region traded gold and slaves.

In 1458, Henry launched his fourth attack on the Moors. He forced a fortress near Tangier to surrender, but it was his last episode of glory: he fell ill and died at Sagres in 1460, the same year his navigator Pedro de Sintra reached the coast of present-day Sierra Leone. His death marked the end of the first great era of Portuguese exploration.

The most detailed contemporary accounts of Henry's life and deeds are those of Zurara, the court chronicler, and of Diogo Gomes, who dictated his memoirs to mapmaker Martin Behaim in the Azores during the 1480s. Henry's own papers—his correspondence and private map collection, as well as the journals and pilot charts of his navigators—were removed in 1470 from Sagres to the court archives in Lisbon, where they were tightly guarded to prevent other nations from learning Portugal's navigational and trade secrets. In later years, thousands of letters, captains' logs, maps, reports, and other documents relating to Portuguese exploration were stored there as well. This entire priceless archive was lost when a massive earthquake destroyed much of Lisbon in 1755.

History remembers King João's third son as Prince Henry the Navigator, yet he made only four sea voyages in his life, and those were short trips through well-known waters. He never visited any of the islands or coastlines that his men explored, and he was not called "the Navigator" until centuries after his death; the title was coined by R. H. Major, a 19th-century British historian. Yet even so, Prince Henry deserves credit for ushering in Europe's greatest era of seagoing exploration, the era that was to produce such master mariners as Christopher Columbus, Ferdinand Magellan, and Sir Francis Drake, for it was Henry who

Among the casualties of the great Lisbon earthquake of 1755 were most of the records and documents pertaining to Portugal's maritime endeavors during its great age of exploration. In the 15th and 16th centuries, Portugal regarded information about the voyages of its mariners as some of its most valuable state secrets.

organized and funded the first enterprise of sustained, systematic exploration, in which scholars and craftsmen from many disciplines worked toward a common goal and each new venture built upon the success or failure of previous efforts, and it was Henry, as foretold at his birth, who prodded the Portuguese into leaving the doorstep of Europe and venturing out into the unknown.

Along an Unknown Coast

Following Prince Henry's death in 1460, Portugal let its exploratory efforts lapse for a few years while King Afonso busied himself with internal politics and crusades against the Moors. Portuguese vessels continued to ply the waters off the African coast, but now they were trading in gold, ivory, and slaves, not exploring new territory. When exploration did resume, it was urged on not by a visionary but by a businessman.

Afonso needed money, and Fernão Gomes, a prosperous Lisbon merchant, needed a business advantage. Gomes offered to buy a monopoly on the Guinea trade from the king. In 1469, Afonso and Gomes made a deal: Gomes agreed to pay an annual fee and to turn over a share of his profits to the Crown in exchange for the king's agreement not to allow anyone else to sail the Guinea coast. Gomes also promised to explore, starting from Sierra Leone, at least 100 leagues—between 300 and 400 miles—of new coastline each year. Exploration and business had become one.

Though his motives may have been mercantile, Gomes proved his worth as an explorer—or, rather, as a master of explorers. By the time his contract with King Afonso expired five years later, his ships and captains had pioneered 2,000 miles of new coastline. It had taken Prince Henry's mariners 40 years to explore the same distance along Africa's shores.

The mythical Christian monarch Prester John, depicted on horseback in this 15th-century Portuguese illustration, inspired many expeditions of exploration by Europeans. The legend of Prester John began in about 1165, when a letter allegedly penned by the mysterious king began circulating throughout Europe's courts.

The first expedition Gomes sent out sailed almost 600 miles past Cape Verde. Once his mariners had rounded Cape Palmas on the present-day border of Liberia and the Ivory Coast, they found the coast ahead of them trending straightaway to the east, and they grew jubilant at the thought that perhaps they had reached the bottom of Africa. It was at this time that people began to speak of a possible sea route around Africa to the Indies.

In voyage after dogged voyage, Gomes's captains pushed on. They brought back cargoes of slaves, ivory, and gold. Along the coast of present-day Benin they discovered a type of pepper, which, while not as highly prized as Asian pepper, gave Portugal an entry into the spice trade. With every advance they built forts, supply bases, and trading posts, stringing a necklace of Portuguese outposts ever farther along the African coast.

In 1473, Gomes's captain Fernando Pó returned to Portugal with bad news. He had passed the mouth of the Niger River, carefully making his way past the labyrinth of channels and sandbanks where the river meets the sea, and penetrated to the eastern end of the Gulf of Guinea. There he found, to his chagrin, that the coast once again turned sharply south, with no end in sight. It seemed that the Portuguese had not reached the bottom of Africa after all, only the bottom of its great western bulge. But the notion of discovering an eastern seaway to India remained.

The European image of the world had greatly changed since the early years of the century, when Prince Henry established himself at Sagres to study geography. Fra Mauro and other mapmakers had questioned Ptolemy's claim that Africa extended southward all the way around the globe and connected with Asia, closing the Indian Ocean off so that it could not be reached from the Atlantic Ocean. Furthermore, a traveler had returned from Asia with new information. He was Niccolò de' Conti, a Venetian who had wandered Asia from 1419 to 1444. His travels had taken him from the Arabian Peninsula to India, Ceylon,

Sumatra, Burma, and Java, but it was his speculation that it was most likely possible to reach the Spice Islands by sailing south and east around Africa that truly excited Europeans. This surmise was seized upon by mapmakers, geographers, captains, and kings, who made plans to test it in practice.

Portugal took a keen interest in these developments. As Pope Nicholas V had granted control of all sea traffic along the West African coast to Portugal in 1454, the seaway to India—if it existed—would clearly be in Portuguese hands. From the time of Gomes's contract, the desire to find a new, direct route to the Indies played an ever-increasing part in the Portuguese enterprise of exploration.

There was another motive as well, one that had been present in Prince Henry's time but gained importance in the second half of the 15th century. It concerned a mythical monarch and his legendary kingdom.

Prester John was a legend who would not die. Since the middle of the 12th century, the people of Europe had been tantalized by rumors of a Christian king who ruled a powerful and wealthy kingdom somewhere outside the known world. The king's name was Prester John. For a time his realm was thought to be in India or Central Asia, where colonies of Christians had been established long before. When Prester John's kingdom continually eluded the travelers and envoys who went searching for it, mapmakers began placing it in the heart of East Africa, and over time it became loosely identified with Abyssinia, or Ethiopia, which was a remote kingdom ruled by a Christian king. Zurara mentions that one reason Prince Henry sent ships into the unknown was to find Prester John, who would presumably be a stout ally against the Muslims. The search for Prester John continued for many years after Henry's death.

Fernão Gomes's lease on the Guinea trade expired in 1474, the same year that his captain Rui de Sequeira reached and crossed the equator. Instead of renewing

Pope Nicholas V granted control of all sea traffic along the west coast of Africa to Portugal in 1454. The names the Portuguese assigned the discoveries of their mariners there—the Ivory Coast, the Slave Coast, the Gold Coast— indicate the source of the wealth their explorations brought the homeland.

Gomes's pact, King Afonso awarded the trade and exploration rights in Africa to his son João, who was interested in geography and navigation. When João became king of Portugal in 1481, he immediately launched a new, vigorous era of exploration, with the clear goal of reaching the Indies by way of Africa. According to the historian Peter Forbath, author of *The River Congo*, João "made the West African enterprise the top priority of his reign and set it the specific tasks of exploiting the Guinea trade to its fullest, circumnavigating the African continent and breaking into the Indies trade, establishing an overseas Portuguese empire, and finding Prester John."

One of João's first acts was to assemble a group of advisers, as Henry had done. This council included the royal physician and mathematician, a bishop, and a Jewish scholar named José Vizinho, whose teacher, Abraham Zacuto, would join him in Lisbon a decade later. These and other learned men worked on a set of tables and rules for calculating latitude, and they also devised improvements in navigational equipment—compasses and hourglasses, for example, were made more accurate and easier to use. All of these resources were placed at the disposal of King João's first captain, Diogo Cão, the scion of a family with a long history of seafaring.

Cão was also supplied with an innovation of João's called the *padrão*. Before Cão, Portuguese captains had signified their arrival at a new landmark or stretch of coastline by scratching marks on trees or by setting up crosses made of wood. João thought that these symbols were neither regal nor durable enough to mark Portugal's claims, so he ordered his stonemasons to produce marble pillars, each some five feet tall. The top of each pillar was a cube on which was carved the royal arms of Portugal, with a cross above them. Cão was given a number of these padrões and ordered to erect them at prominent spots in new territory.

Many of Prince Henry's early expeditions had been captained by ambitious but untried aristocratic youths. Cão

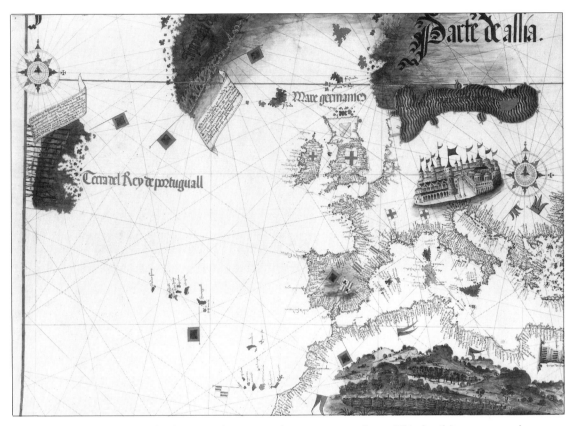

This detail from an ornately illustrated Portuguese padron (a map of the world on which all new discoveries were officially recorded) shows its island discoveries and its claims in northwest Africa as well as the Mediterranean world from which oceangoing Portugal was turning away.

was a different breed of sea explorer: tough, experienced, practical, and businesslike. He set out at once, in May or June 1482, and wasted no time in passing Sequeira's farthest-south. He then began inching his way southward along an unknown and difficult shore—the coast of present-day Gabon and the Congo Republic.

The current and winds were against him. The weather was bad; thunderstorms and rain squalls made navigation difficult, and the stupefying equatorial heat sapped the men's strength. There were few good anchorages along the silent shore, which consisted of red clay cliffs topped by impenetrable dark green forests. The water was shallow a long way out from land, and to avoid running aground, Cão had to remain as much as 15 miles offshore, studying the distant coastline through his telescope.

One day Cão came upon a large bay, where the cliffs fell away and the shoreline opened into a wide, sandy arc, lined by dark, tangled mangrove swamps and tall palms. A blue-gray shimmer on the horizon hinted at mountains deep in the interior. The water of the bay was a muddy yellowish brown, and when Cão sailed closer he felt a strong current rushing out to sea. He lowered a bucket and tasted the water: it was not salty. Cão had discovered not a bay but the mouth of a mighty river—the Congo (sometimes called the Zaire), the second longest river in Africa and the fifth longest in the world. If the river proved navigable, Cão realized at once, it would be an open highway into the heart of Africa.

Cão took his ship into the river's mouth and sailed slowly and cautiously upstream. His men gazed in wonder at the thick forest all around, the flocks of bright, noisy parrots, the crocodiles lazing on the sandbanks. Soon people stepped out of the forest to watch the ship's advance. A few miles upstream, Cão landed in a cove and ordered the men to raise one of King João's padrões. Centuries later, the pillar was found on that spot, with its inscription still legible:

> In the year 6681 of the World and in that of 1482 since the birth of our Lord Jesus Christ, the most serene, the most excellent and potent prince, King João II of Portugal did order this land discovered and this pillar of stone to be erected by Diogo Cão, an esquire in his household.

Cão remained at the Congo mouth for some time, probably a month or more. He and his men established friendly relations with the local people, and gradually the Portuguese and the natives—who called themselves the Bakongo—learned to communicate with one another. The Bakongo told Cão that they were ruled by a powerful king called the Manikongo, whose royal city lay some distance upriver. This was electrifying news: had Cão finally discovered the whereabouts of Prester John and his mysterious kingdom? Leaving behind several of his men with orders to travel upstream in search of the Manikongo, Cão set off southward once more. At a headland that he named Cape St. Mary, about 500 miles south of the Congo on the coast of present-day Angola, he erected another padrão, then returned to the Congo. As his men had not yet returned from the interior, he took several Bakongo hostage and went back to Portugal, where he arrived in the spring of 1484.

His return caused a sensation. Not only had Cão discovered a huge river and added about 1,000 miles of new coastline to the map of Africa, but he had found a clue to Prester John's location. Instead of being enslaved, the four Bakongo he brought home were treated as ambassadors, housed in King João's palace, and outfitted by the royal tailors. The king intended to send them back to their homeland, and he wanted them to tell the Manikongo about his kindness, friendliness, and prosperity.

There was another reason for the interest that Cão's voyage aroused throughout Europe, for it was rumored that he had actually sailed around Africa and found an open seaway to the Indies. The rumor gained strength when the king ordered that the details of Cão's voyage be kept a strict secret. Modern historians are certain that Cão did not reach the southern tip of Africa, but the very existence of the rumor indicates a widespread belief that such a discovery was imminent.

João sent Cão out again in 1485 with three ships. This time, the mariner was under orders to press southward until he rounded Africa. On the way, Cão stopped at the Congo to release the four Bakongo "ambassadors" and to pick up the men he had left on his earlier visit. While awaiting the arrival of his men from the Manikongo's court, Cão sailed one of his caravels as far upriver as the present-day city of Matadi, where he carved his name into a cliff. At a place where the river foams through a narrow gorge, his progress was halted by impassable waterfalls and rapids.

Christopher Columbus lands on Hispaniola in 1492 and is offered lavish gifts by the unclad native inhabitants of the New World in this early-16th-century woodcut. King João II's commitment to reaching Asia by sailing east, around Africa's southern tip, led him to forgo an opportunity to invest in Columbus's Enterprise of the Indies, a decision that, despite the success of his own mariners, he later came to regret. "Why did I let slip such a wonderful chance?" João reportedly lamented aloud when Columbus reported his success at the Portuguese court on his return from Hispaniola.

At this point, the accounts of Cão's second voyage become confused. According to one story, he sailed out of the Congo and on to the south, reaching a point on the desert coast of present-day Namibia before returning to Portugal. Furious that Cão had not rounded Africa, King João ordered the navigator banished from the court. Another version of the story says that Cão perished along that southern shore. The truth may never be known, for Cão's name vanishes from the histories after his second visit to the mouth of the Congo. Nothing is recorded of his later life, the manner of his death, or his place of burial, although the men he sent to visit the Manikongo did reach Portugal by 1488. Either Cão brought them back, or they came back in his ships after his death, or they were picked up and returned to Lisbon by the next Portuguese mariner to explore the African coast, Bartolomeu Dias de Novais. All that is known for certain of Cão's final voyage is that he reached a new farthest-south some 700 miles south of Cape St. Mary. He called this place Cape Cross, and

there he raised a padrão that marked the spot for hundreds of years.

Between Cão's two voyages, King João received an interesting offer from a Genoese sailor who had been living in Portugal for some years. In Portuguese, this sailor's name was Cristovao Colom, but history remembers him as Christopher Columbus. He had conceived a plan that he called the Enterprise of the Indies, and he wanted João to sponsor it.

Columbus believed that he could reach Japan, China, and the Indies by sailing west instead of east. Like all educated Europeans, he knew that the world is round, although his calculations led him to believe that it was quite a bit smaller than it really is. He thought that the distance from the Canary Islands to Japan must be about 2,500 miles, when in fact it is more than 10,000 miles. Of course, he also had no idea that two large, unknown continents barred the way. He offered to find a western route to the Indies and claim it for Portugal, if João would supply him with the necessary ships and men.

João referred the matter to his advisers—including Cão, who was between voyages at the time. On their recommendation, he turned Columbus down. The Portuguese recognized that in theory one could sail west to Asia, but they felt that Columbus's calculations were wrong and that the actual journey would be too long for anyone to endure. In addition, Portugal had already spent 65 years and a great deal of money on African exploration, and João, encouraged by Cão's first voyage, was convinced that a route east around Africa was within his grasp. Eventually, Columbus sold the Spanish monarchs Ferdinand and Isabella on the Enterprise of the Indies, and the result was the European discovery of the Americas and the foundation of Spain's empire in the New World. By that time, however, King João had developed an ambitious plan to solve once and for all the mysteries of Prester John and the passage to the Indies.

The Conquest
of the Cape

King João II planned a two-part reconnaissance to resolve the question of the India passage. After careful preparation, in 1487 the king sent out a pair of expeditions, one by sea and the other by land.

The captain of the seaward venture, Bartolomeu Dias de Novais, has been enshrined in generations of schoolbooks as one of the heroes of the age of exploration. Yet the men who made the landward journey—Pero da Covilhã and Afonso de Paiva—are virtually unknown today, though their experiences were as harrowing and their contributions as important as those of Dias.

Covilhã, who was in his twenties when his long journey began, seems to have been an extraordinarily capable and versatile man. He spoke many languages, including Arabic, and had served as João's spy both in the Spanish court and with the Moors in North Africa. Little is known about Paiva, a Portuguese courtier, except that he also spoke Arabic.

On May 7, 1487, King João presented Covilhã and Paiva with engraved medallions, a map, and secret instructions, said farewell, and sent them on their way. They first went east, stopping in the Spanish city of Barcelona, the Italian city of Naples, and the Greek island of Rhodes before, disguised as Muslim merchants trying to sell a cargo of honey, they arrived in the Egyptian port of Alexandria, the Mediterranean gateway to the Arab empire. From there they went to Cairo, and then on to Aden, on the Red Sea.

A Nile River scene, from a 2nd-century Italian mosaic. By the 15th century, East Africa had generally been fixed by Europeans as the likely dwelling-place of the elusive Prester John, so Pero da Covilhã and Afonso de Paiva began their explorations in Egypt.

Covilhã was not disappointed by the Arab marketplaces he visited on the Arabian Peninsula, the Malabar Coast, and the east coast of Africa.

At Aden they separated. Paiva's orders were to go south, into the mountains of Abyssinia, to make contact with Prester John. Covilhã, meanwhile, was to make his way to India and discover as much as possible about the spice trade—in effect, to become a geography and trade spy. He took passage on a ship across the Arabian Sea and reached the southwestern coast of India, where he spent time in the large, busy trading ports of Goa and Calicut. He witnessed shiploads of goods arriving from the more remote East: pungent spices from the Moluccas, elegant Chinese porcelain vases, sumptuous silks and brocades, also from China. He saw the flourishing trade in horses from Arabia and Iran, and he also saw gold and ivory arriving from the east coast of Africa. By talking with sailors and merchants, Covilhã picked up a fair knowledge of the Indies trade, which he immediately recognized was even more sophisticated and varied than had been supposed in Europe; he also learned about such navigational matters as the monsoons, or seasonal winds, of the Indian Ocean.

Covilhã remained in India until February 1489, when he sailed back across the Arabian Sea to the port of Hormuz at the entrance of the Persian Gulf. Still passing himself off as a Muslim trader, he then traveled down the east coast of Africa in Arab dhows as far south as Sofala, in present-day Mozambique, which was the southernmost Arab trading post in southeast Africa.

In 1490, he made his way back to Cairo, where he learned that Paiva had died of a fever. Awaiting him were fresh orders from King João, dispatching him to Abyssinia in order to complete Paiva's mission. By this time, Covilhã had been away from his wife and children for three years, but the king's orders took precedence over homesickness. After writing João a long letter in which he reported everything he had learned about the ports, harbors, and trade routes of the Indian Ocean, he resumed his undercover work. Disguised as a Muslim pilgrim, he visited Mecca and Medina, the holy cities of Islam, in present-day

Saudi Arabia; he is the first European known to have done so. Then, in about 1493, he set out for Abyssinia.

Covilhã succeeded in reaching the court of the Abyssinian emperor, Alexander, Lion of the Tribe of Judah and King of Kings, but he did not succeed in getting away again. Although the emperor always treated foreign visitors kindly, he did not permit them to leave. When Portuguese ambassadors arrived in Abyssinia 30 years later, they found Covilhã still there, living a luxurious but confined life and married to a local woman.

His letter reached King João in 1490 or 1491. Although the document itself has not survived, it is known to have contained much information that the Portuguese found useful when they began establishing an empire in the Indian Ocean. (It was Covilhã's report, for example, that told Vasco da Gama what to expect on the east coast of Africa.) Together with the results of Dias's sea voyage, it convinced the Portuguese that they could reach the Indies by way of Africa.

Dias began his journey in the fall of 1487, a few months after Covilhã and Paiva left Portugal. Nothing is known about Dias except that he had been active in the shipment of ivory from Guinea to Portugal in the late 1470s and that in 1481 he commanded a caravel on a voyage to Elmina, the principal Portuguese fortress and trading post on the Gulf of Guinea. He was, therefore, familiar with both caravels and the African coast.

He appears to have planned his trip intelligently. Not only did he take the two caravels granted by King João, but he added a third ship to carry supplies for the other two, as Cão's description of the desolation of Africa's southwest coast made him think it unlikely that he could obtain food or water there. The use of a storeship made it possible for him to stay away from port longer and go farther; the tactic was copied by many later mariners, including Gama.

In addition to his crew, Dias carried six African passengers—four women and two men—who had been

Among the enticing riches to be found in the East, Covilhã reported to João in his famous letter to the king, was silk, which is produced by silkworms in spinning their cocoons. These women are reeling in the delicate fiber from the cocoons. Silk from the Far East had been prized as a luxury in Europe since before the time of Christ.

brought to Portugal by earlier explorers. On João's orders, the Africans were dressed and equipped like Europeans and supplied with samples of trade goods. Dias was to leave them at various points along his route. The king hoped that they would carry his regards to Prester John, or at least arouse the interest of their fellow Africans in trading with the Europeans.

Dias bypassed the Gulf of Guinea, sailing directly from Cape Palmas to the mouth of the Congo. From there he sailed along the coast until he had reached Cão's farthest-south at Cape Cross. By this time he was having trouble making headway against the stiff winds and strong currents from the south, so he left the clumsy storeship in a sheltered bay on the coast of present-day South Africa and went on, battling his way southward at an agonizingly slow rate. What happened next has been interpreted several ways.

For reasons that remain unknown, Dias's ships stood away from land and headed out into the open sea, where they made a wide curve to the south. Some sources believe that they were blown offshore in a gale; others claim that Dias made a bold and imaginative decision to stand away from shore in the hope of escaping the troublesome southerly winds and currents. If the first interpretation is true, Dias was simply lucky; if the second is correct, he was a nautical genius.

The most likely explanation is that the ships were struck by a gale and that Dias, instead of fighting the storm, decided to ride it out to sea and let it carry him south. After 13 days, the ships picked up a wind from the west—part of the wind belt called the westerlies that blows eternally around the planet's southern latitudes. The vessels were carried east on this wind for days, while the men fretted about the size of the waves and the coldness of the water, which was chilled by the icebergs of unknown Antarctica, below the southern horizon. Finally, Dias gave the order to steer north, and a few days later the Portuguese sighted land on the horizon. As the ships approached the mountainous coastline, Dias noted that it did not run from north to

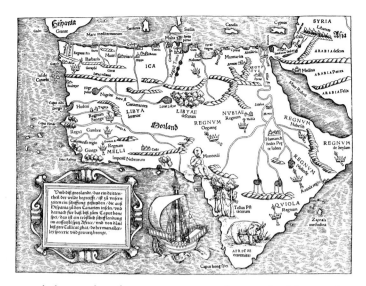

This map from Sebastian Münster's Cosmography, *published in 1544, illustrates the European conception of the continent of Africa several decades after Bartolomeu Dias had succeeded in rounding its southernmost cape. Belief in the existence of Prester John had persisted; his castle is depicted near the fork of the upper branches of the Nile.*

south but rather from west to east: he was looking at the southern coast of Africa, the goal of so many questing navigators. He had reached the bottom of the continent.

Dias owed his success to that wide arc out into the south Atlantic Ocean. By accident or design, he had happened upon the most efficient way for a sailing vessel to round Africa: out into the middle of the ocean, away from the southerly winds and currents of the coast, south to the westerly belt, and then east and up. This course has been followed by sailing craft ever since Dias's day.

Farther away from home than any vessels that ever had flown the flag of their nation, the two ships put in on February 3, 1488, at an anchorage that is now called Mossel Bay, then proceeded northeast along the coast until Dias was quite sure that he had reached the eastern coast of Africa. At the mouth of the Great Fish River, Dias erected a padrão—the same marker seen by Vasco da Gama a decade later.

Legend has it that Dias was determined to go on all the way to India but that his men threatened mutiny and forced him to turn back. "Weary, and terrified of the great seas through which they had passed, all with one voice began to murmur, and demand that they proceed no farther," wrote João de Barros, a 16th-century Portuguese historian who penned one of the few accounts of Dias's voyage in his monumental chronicle *Décadas da Asia*, which recounts the story of Portuguese exploration.

The reality was probably less dramatic. It was not unusual for officers and crew members to make their views known, especially in the case of a small fleet on an exploratory mission. The ships were in poor shape, with torn sails and frayed rigging; food and water were running low, and no one knew whether provisions could be found along the coast ahead. When it became clear that most of the men wanted to turn back, Dias asked them to sign a paper to that effect—very likely he was afraid that the king would be angry with him for not pressing on to India. Then he ordered the ships to turn about and head for home. He had added 1,260 miles of new coastline to the map.

On the way back around the southern coast of Africa, Dias sighted a high, imposing promontory thrusting out into the sea, where the blue southern ocean broke into white waves that crashed against its rocky base and the white-sand beaches on either side. He determined that this was the uttermost tip of Africa and named it Cabo Tormen-

This ornately embellished Portuguese padron depicts the horn of Africa, the Arabian Peninsula, the Indian subcontinent, and the Spice Islands—the lands several generations of Portuguese mariners aspired to reach. The wonder these exotic places held for the Portuguese is evident in the attention the artist has devoted to their flora, fauna, architecture, and human inhabitants.

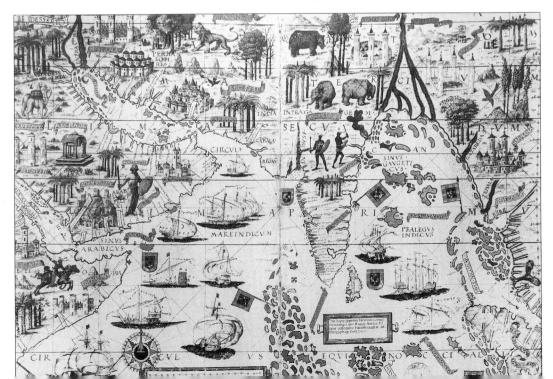

toso, or the Cape of Storms, because of the gale winds that had kept him from seeing it on the outward journey.

At the bay where he had left the storeship, Dias discovered that most of the men he had left there had died, either from hunger, from disease, or from fighting with the natives. He picked up the handful of survivors and went on. He stopped at least twice more, once at an island in the Gulf of Guinea to rescue a Portuguese shipwreck survivor and once at Elmina to pick up the season's take of gold dust for transport to Portugal; it is possible that a third stop was made near the mouth of the Congo to pick up the survivors of Cão's second expedition, as some sources say that when the two caravels reached Lisbon in December 1488, they carried several Africans sent by the Manikongo, the mysterious king of the Congo. (One of these African envoys, who may very well have reached Portugal with Cão or an unknown captain, later became rather well known at the Portuguese court. His name was Nsaku. He learned Portuguese and then decided to become a Christian; King João himself attended his baptism and christened him Dom João da Silva, or Sir John of the Forest.)

Dias was well received by the king, who apparently did not blame him for not having reached India. Indeed, João listened with great interest and delight to Dias's report that Africa had at last been rounded. Columbus, who was in Portugal at the time, trying again to sell his Enterprise of the Indies to King João, later claimed to have been present when Dias made his report. If so, he must have realized dispiritedly that now, more than ever, the Portuguese would care nothing for his westward venture. All their attention would be turned eastward.

Dias had proved that a sea route existed around the southern edge of Africa; now it only remained to be proved that the seaway lay open all the way to India. King João had such high expectations for this route that he gave a new name to the promontory that Dias had called the Cape of Storms. João dubbed it the Cape of Good Hope.

An Empire
in the East

Despite the excitement generated by Dias's achievement, King João II did not immediately dispatch a follow-
up expedition. Nearly a decade would pass before Vasco da
Gama sailed south in Dias's wake on the sea road to India.

Historians have suggested several reasons for the delay.
João was probably waiting to receive Covilhã's report on
the Indies trade, which did not arrive until several years
after Dias's return, and the king was ill, increasingly debi-
litated by a progressive and painful kidney disease that was
to kill him in 1495. The last few years of his rule were
troubled by internal dissension, the death of his only son,
and growing hostility between Portugal and Spain.

Much of that hostility concerned matters of geography
and exploration. Portugal and Spain were competing to
reach the Indies and gain control of the spice trade. Within
the span of a few years in the 1480s and 1490s, the two
nations launched expeditions that added much new territory to the map of the world, and then they carved that
world up between them.

Portugal's claim to leadership in the exploration of the
African coast was unquestioned, but in 1493 Christopher
Columbus, having won the support of Spain for his Enterprise of the Indies, returned from a voyage to the western reaches of the Atlantic, where he had found tropical
islands, natives, and gold. Initially, everyone believed
those islands to be the outer limits of the Indies, but in
time others began to realize that Columbus had stumbled

*By 1500, the ships of Spain and
Portugal had essentially divided
the oceans between them. The
competition between the Iberian
rivals to find a sea route to the
Indies gave Spain a New World
and Portugal a new empire.*

upon unexpected lands in the western sea: the Americas. But even before the geography of the New World was fully understood, Spain and Portugal hastened to stake their rival claims.

As the discoverer of the eastward route around Africa, Portugal felt it had earned the right to control trade with the Indies along that route. The Spanish, on the other hand, had taken a chance on Columbus and felt that they deserved to benefit from the westward route he had opened. As European nations of that time were accustomed to submitting political as well as spiritual matters to the authority of the Vatican, King João of Portugal and King Ferdinand and Queen Isabella of Spain agreed to let the pope settle their claims. In 1494 Pope Alexander VI proclaimed the Treaty of Tordesillas, in which he did his best to please both sides.

The treaty divided the world along an imaginary line down the middle of the Atlantic Ocean about 2,300 miles west of the Cape Verde Islands. Portugal was granted the sole right to explore and trade east of that line and to claim any new lands that were discovered there; Spain was given

Pope Alexander VI (left), the promulgator of the Treaty of Tordesillas, was a Spaniard by birth, but Portugal regarded his mediation of its dispute with Spain over the two nations' maritime discoveries as fair.

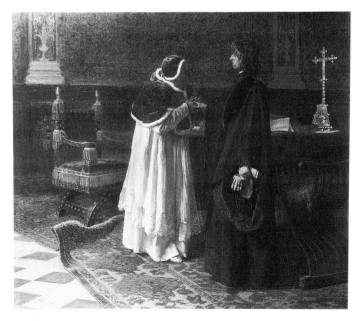

dominion over everything west of the line. In essence, the treaty confirmed Portugal's control of the Guinea trade and the sea route around Africa while it established Spain's sovereignty in the western Atlantic. At first the Spanish understood this to mean that they would be able to sail west to the easternmost part of the Indies. Later, when the Americas were recognized as previously unknown continents, the Spanish interpreted the Treaty of Tordesillas as their exclusive claim to the New World. The only part of the Americas that did not belong to Spain under the Treaty of Tordesillas was the eastward bulge of South America, where Brazil is located. This region was eventually claimed by Portugal. The wishes of the native inhabitants of these new lands were not considered.

Once the treaty was settled, Portugal could proceed with its plans for an expedition to India. One of King João's last acts was to appoint a captain for the expedition. For reasons unknown, he passed over Bartolomeu Dias for the assignment and chose Vasco da Gama instead. Dias was assigned to give Gama advice and to design his ships, a task he apparently performed without complaint. It was Dias who recommended that Gama's fleet stand well out from land in the South Atlantic to pick up the westerlies, and Dias also suggested that Gama's ships should be *naus* rather than caravels because the larger ships were more suitable for open-sea sailing. The *São Gabriel* and the *São Rafael* were built to his specifications, with square sails to catch the following winds and shallow drafts to pick their way through inshore channels.

When João succumbed at last to his illness in 1495, his nephew Manoel became king. Manoel's councillors advised him to cancel the expedition, fearing that it might stir up trouble with Venice, the European controller of the spice trade, but the new king overruled his timid council and ordered the preparations to continue.

While Dias worked on the ships, Gama studied Covilhã's report and other sources of information about Africa and

India. Because so many records were lost in the 1755 Lisbon earthquake, not much is known about Gama's early life or his preparation for the voyage. Even the year of his birth is unknown, although tradition says that he was born in 1460, the year of Prince Henry's death. His father was the governor of Sines, a fishing port in southern Portugal, and the Gamas belonged to the minor nobility. Vasco da Gama is thought to have carried out some diplomatic missions for the king, although there is no record of his having commanded a ship before the trip to the Indies.

When Gama's fleet set off from Lisbon in July 1497, Dias sailed with it as far as the Cape Verde Islands. He was to take up an administrative post on the Guinea coast, but it is hard not to wonder what he thought as he stood on the dock and watched Gama's little fleet vanish over the southern horizon on its way to attempt the passage he had discovered.

Gama then made his historic open-sea voyage to the Cape, rounded Africa, and began to work his way up the east coast. There followed the suffering from scurvy, the wrangling with local sultans and pilots, and the crossing of the Arabian Sea. Finally, in May 1498, Gama's fleet sailed into the harbor at Calicut, which Covilhã had called one of the chief ports of the Malabar Coast. Having reached India, Gama now had to gain a foothold in the spice trade if his mission was to be deemed a success.

As soon as the ships were anchored, the captain-major sent one of the expendable convicts into Calicut to investigate the situation. The first people the felon met were two North African Muslims who spoke several Mediterranean languages. One of these fellows returned to the ships with the convict and greeted the captain-major in Portuguese. "We were greatly astonished," says the author of the *Roteiro*, "for we never expected to hear our language spoken so far away from Portugal." What the men said excited the Portuguese as much as the language it was spoken in. "A lucky venture, a lucky venture! Plenty of rubies, plenty of emeralds! You owe great thanks to God for having brought you to a country holding such riches!" the *Roteiro* records the North Africans as saying.

Despite this unexpected touch of familiarity, much of what the Portuguese encountered in India was utterly strange, and it is not surprising that they misunderstood many things. They seem to have had no knowledge at all of the ancient, complex Hindu religion and to have been convinced that the Hindus they met were members of some strange Christian sect. Upon visiting a temple, which they called a chapel, they saw what they thought were portraits of saints on the wall. The author of the *Roteiro* noted somewhat uneasily that the saints had long, protruding teeth and four or five arms—features commonly found in images of certain Hindu deities.

About one thing, however, the Portuguese made no mistake. India was as rich with trade possibilities as Europe had always dreamed. The *Roteiro* dwells lovingly on a description of the gold jewelry, ornaments, and even spittoons possessed by the *zamorin*, the local Hindu ruler. The Portuguese also saw many pearls and precious stones, as well as Arab vessels in the harbor taking on bales of costly spices and silks, but they found themselves unable to participate in this inviting commerce, for they had brought with them only cheap cloth and trinkets such as bells and mirrors—trade goods that were popular with the natives of West Africa but failed to impress the wealthy, sophisticated Indian Ocean merchants. Indeed, when Gama offered some of these goods as a courtesy gift to the zamorin, the ruler was insulted. Though Gama was able to obtain some samples of spices and other Indian merchandise—ginger, cinnamon, pepper, cloves, nutmeg, and a handful of jewels—he did so at a loss.

Matters were complicated by the hostility the Portuguese faced from the Muslim merchants who controlled the Indian Ocean trade. These merchants wanted no competition, and they tried to turn the zamorin against Gama. When one of the friendly North Africans warned Gama that there was a plot against his life, the captain-major

Da Gama delivers a letter from King Manoel to the zamorin of Calicut, who was not impressed by the explanation of the Portuguese that they had come, according to the Roteiro, *"merely to make discoveries . . . not because they sought gold or silver, for of this they had such abundance that they needed not what was to be found in this country."*

decided that he could accomplish nothing more in Calicut. Upon hearing that the Portuguese were leaving, the zamorin confiscated their trade goods and took several hostages. Though the captives were eventually returned, Gama detained several Indian prisoners, whom he planned to take back to Portugal.

The zamorin did agree to erect one of Gama's stone pillars, and he gave the captain-major a letter to take back to King Manoel. Written with an iron pen on a palm leaf, the letter read:

> Vasco da Gama, a gentleman of your household, came to my country, whereat I was pleased. My country is rich in cinnamon, cloves, ginger, pepper, and precious stones. That which I ask of you in return is gold, silver, corals, and scarlet cloth.

On August 29, Gama sailed for home, but he had departed too early for the favorable winds, and this time the crossing of the Arabian Sea took about three months. By the time the fleet reached Malindi, so many crewmen were ill with scurvy that they could no longer manage three vessels, and Gama ordered the *São Rafael* burned. Its crew found places aboard the two remaining ships, which made their way down the African coast and rounded the Cape on March 20, 1499.

The *Berrio* arrived in Lisbon to great rejoicing on July 10. Gama, however, paused in the Azores, west of Portugal, where his brother Paulo died. He did not reach Lisbon in the *São Gabriel* until September. His homeland welcomed him with rapturous praise, while the other nations of Europe viewed his return with mingled envy and alarm. King Manoel wrote at once to the Spanish king and queen, boasting that he had beaten the Spanish to India. He took to calling himself, grandly but rather inaccurately, "Lord of Guinea and of the Conquest, Navigation, and Commerce of Ethiopia, Arabia, Persia, and India." In fulfillment of his vow, he ordered construction to begin on the glorious church of São Jeronimo in Lisbon.

In truth, the immediate diplomatic and commercial consequences of Vasco da Gama's mission were somewhat disappointing. He had failed to make much of an impression on the rulers he had met, he had failed to negotiate any treaties or trading concessions, and he had not even brought back a profitable cargo. But, unlike Columbus, Gama had actually reached the Indies, the longtime dream of most European nations, and the long-term significance of the journey was far greater than its immediate returns. On the foundation of Gama's voyage, Portugal would build an empire in the East.

The trip did produce substantial immediate benefits for its captain-major, who was luckier than Cão, Dias, and many other explorers whose efforts went unrewarded. The king granted Gama a title, a large pension, and an estate, making Gama one of the few explorers in the great age of European discovery to profit significantly from his explorations.

Gama's return from Calicut introduced a new phase of Portuguese exploration. India, the goal for many years, had been found. From now on, Portuguese exploration would be concerned not so much with discovery as with conquest, colonization, and commerce, as was already the case along the Guinea coast. Having discovered the sea path to Asia, Portugal now wanted to become a power there.

King Manoel lost no time in fitting out a fleet to return to India. As its purpose was not investigation but conquest, the fleet was massive: it consisted of 13 ships and 1,200 men—about one-tenth of one percent of Portugal's total population. Pedro Álvares Cabral, a nobleman with no known experience at sea or abroad, was appointed its commander; Gama, who supported the choice of Cabral, provided the neophyte mariner with navigation tips. One of Cabral's ships was captained by Bartolomeu Dias, who was finally being permitted to travel the route that he had pioneered, although not as the supreme commander. (Dias never did reach India, however; his ship was one of several that were lost in a storm at sea.)

Cabral's armada set sail from the Tagus River on March 9, 1500. On Gama's advice, Cabral swung his fleet wide of the African coast in a vast arc that carried him south and west; so far west that in late April his ships sighted land dead ahead—the large eastward-thrusting bulge of South America, just north of the present-day site of Rio de Janeiro, Brazil. As his was not intended to be a voyage of discovery, Cabral had no padrões to plant there, but he raised a wooden cross on shore, assigned two convicts to remain in Brazil to gather information about this new land, sent a ship back to Portugal with news of the discovery, and then continued on his way to India. Cabral's accidental encounter with South America won him fame as the European discoverer of Brazil; the fate of the two men left behind is unknown.

Brazil was not the only discovery in store for Cabral's fleet. The ships were separated in a storm, and after rounding the

In wisely emulating his predecessors Dias and Gama by swinging widely away from the west coast of Africa in order to round the Cape of Good Hope, Pedro Álvares Cabral inadvertently discovered Brazil, the eastward bulge of which made it the only part of the Americas to lie on the Portuguese side of the line established by the Treaty of Tordesillas.

A Portuguese armada sets sail from Lisbon in this Theodore de Bry engraving from the 16th century. Although Portugal's savagery in its new outposts never gained it the infamy that Spain received for its cruel New World practices, armed might and terror were essential to Portugal's success in establishing its overseas dominions. According to the historian R. S. Whiteway, "Cruelties were . . . deliberately adopted as a line of terrorizing policy by Vasco da Gama, Almeida and Albuquerque."

Cape of Good Hope, a vessel captained by Lourenço Marques made the first European landing upon Madagascar, a large island off the coast of southeast Africa, and claimed it for Portugal.

Cabral's mission to India was not altogether successful. The zamorin of Calicut refused to cooperate with him, and an angry mob killed some 50 Portuguese. In retaliation, Cabral bombarded the town, earning for the Portuguese the lasting hatred of the Arabs and Indians there and a reputation for brutality that Gama and his successors would do much to affirm. Cabral did succeed, however, in establishing a permanent Portuguese presence in the region, in the form of trading posts at Calicut and Cochin, which is farther south on the Malabar Coast.

Cabral returned to Portugal in the summer of 1501. He had lost more than half his ships and men, but the holds of the returning vessels were filled with pepper, ginger, cinnamon, camphor, cloves, opium, indigo, and other highly prized spices of the East, and the returning men told wonderful tales of the teeming bazaars of the Malabar Coast, bursting with rubies and pearls and all manner of

(continued on page 92)

Voyages To North America

Although the main thrust of Portuguese exploration was directed toward Africa and the Indies, not all of the Portuguese voyages involved tropical seas and palm-fringed coasts. During the early years of the 16th century, men from the Portuguese Azores made several voyages through the stormy gray seas of the North Atlantic to the bleak, fog-enshrouded shores of Greenland and Canada.

In 1499 King Manoel granted permission to João Fernandes and Pedro Maria de Barcelos of Terceira Island in the Azores to look for new islands. Fernandes had visited Britain and doubtless knew of John Cabot's two voyages west across the North Atlantic from Britain in the 1490s. Cabot had sighted land, which he believed to be Asia, and Fernandes and Barcelos decided to examine that part of the world more closely. They sailed in the summer of 1500. Fernandes, who was a *lavrador*, or minor landowner, was the first to sight land—the southern coast of Greenland. In his honor the place was called the Labrador, a name that was later used to delineate the large peninsula in eastern Canada that still bears that appellation.

In 1500, King Manoel allowed another Azorean, Gaspar Côrte-Real, one of his favorite knights, to go adventuring in the North Atlantic. Gaspar crossed the ocean from Lisbon and sighted what his crew later described as "a land that was very cool and with big trees"—almost certainly the island of Newfoundland, which is now part of Canada. In great excitement, he returned to Portugal and fitted out three ships for a more ambitious exploration.

The three ships set sail in May 1501. In October two of them returned to Portugal, with 57 Indians taken from Newfoundland as a gift for King Manoel, but Gaspar Côrte-Real's vessel was missing. The other captains reported that he had gone on to explore the coast south of Newfoundland, but neither Gaspar nor any of his men were ever seen or heard of again. In 1502 his brother Miguel set out for Newfoundland to look for him, but his ship also vanished.

A third Côrte-Real brother, Vasco, asked King Manoel for permission to equip an expedition to search for his missing brothers. The king refused; perhaps he felt that the Côrte-Reals were simply unlucky where Newfoundland was concerned. Having lost two knights from that family, he was unwilling to risk a third, but he did name Vasco Côrte-Real captain of the Terra del Rey de Portugal, as Newfoundland was labeled on Portuguese maps. The title remained in the family for more than 70 years, although none of the later Côrte-Reals ever visited Newfoundland. The captaincy died with Manuel Côrte-Real, the last of the family, who was killed fighting the Moors in 1578, and so did Portugal's claims in Canada.

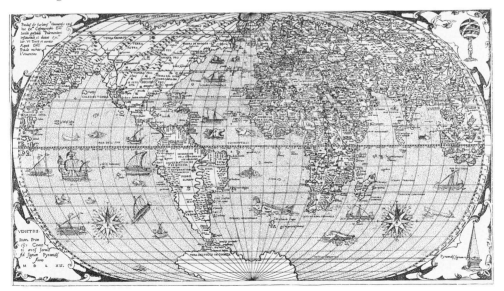

The world as depicted by the Venetian cartographer Gastaldi in 1562, by which time Portugal's mariners had sailed virtually all of its waters.

(continued from page 89)

The Portuguese mariner Tristão (Tristan in English) da Cunha discovered the Tristan da Cunha island group en route to India in the command of a 14-ship fleet that was carrying Afonso de Albuquerque, one of the greatest naval warriors of his day. The Tristan da Cunha group, which consists of five volcanic islands, is in the South Atlantic about midway between South America and South Africa.

desirable things. Portugal rejoiced: the Arab and Venetian stranglehold on the Indies trade had finally been broken.

Gama, now nobly entitled Admiral of the Indian Seas by King Manoel, commanded the next India expedition, which set sail in 1502 for the purpose of establishing Portuguese sovereignty over the East African and Malabar ports. Backed by the guns of 15 ships, Gama enforced this directive mercilessly. He forced the sultan of Kilwa, in present-day Tanzania, to pay tribute, and then he wrought a terrible vengeance on the Muslim world for the deaths of the Portuguese at Calicut by burning a ship that was on its way back to India from Mecca with 380 pilgrims aboard. All the passengers, including numerous women and children, perished; the Portuguese made away with a small fortune in gold coins and trade goods.

At Calicut, Gama demanded that the zamorin expel all Muslims from the city; when the ruler hesitated, the Admiral of the Indian Seas seized a number of fishermen who had been plying the waters of the harbor, hanged and dismembered them, sent their heads and extremities ashore in a boat as a grisly demonstration of the perils of resisting the Portuguese will, and then bombarded the town. Having effectively intimidated rulers and merchants on both sides of the Indian Ocean, Gama then made an extremely favorable trade treaty with the ruler of Cochin, filled his ships with spices, and returned to Portugal in 1503. In the years that followed, he received a share of the profits from every trade voyage to India, an arrangement that made him one of Portugal's richest men.

The Portuguese were now the lords of the sea, and they lost no time in spreading out across their new domain. In 1501–2, on his way to establish new trading posts in India, João da Nova discovered the South Atlantic islands of Ascension and St. Helena; these would later pass into British hands, and St. Helena would become famous as the site of the French emperor Napoléon Bonaparte's exile and death. In 1506, Tristão (Tristan in English) da Cunha discovered the South Atlantic island cluster that today bears his name and also explored part of Madagascar.

But a few isolated islands added little to the wealth of Portugal, and the real focus of the country's maritime enterprises continued to be the conquest of the Indies. In 1505 Francisco de Almeida, named viceroy of India by King Manoel, took a fleet to the Indian Ocean, where he strengthened Portugal's grip on Kilwa and Cochin. One of his junior officers was Ferdinand Magellan, who, in the service of Spain, would later command the fleet that

The greatest Portuguese mariner of the 16th century, Ferdinand Magellan, was sailing for Spain in the course of his epic attempt to circumnavigate the globe when he braved the terrors depicted allegorically here. Magellan left his homeland because he felt that his efforts in helping Portugal secure its overseas empire had gone unappreciated by King Manoel.

The marketplace at Goa, which was Portugal's most important trading outpost on the Malabar Coast of India. The city was secured for Portugal by Albuquerque, who terrorized its populace by sailing into the harbor with corpses dangling from the masts of his ships.

made the first voyage around the world. Magellan was wounded at Almeida's fiercest battle, off the island of Diu, where 1,800 Portuguese in 19 ships defeated a Muslim force of 20,000 men and 2,000 ships.

Almeida's successor as viceroy of India was Afonso de Albuquerque, whose first act was to seize the Malabar port of Goa and order the death of every Arab man, woman, and child in the city. The orgy of systematic slaughter that followed took three days and resulted in more than 8,000 killed, and Goa became the center of Portuguese power in western India. Albuquerque went on to capture the strategically and economically valuable ports of Malacca, on the eastern edge of the Indian Ocean near present-day Singapore, and Hormuz, on the Persian Gulf.

Vasco da Gama spent the years of Almeida's and Albuquerque's viceroyalties at home in Portugal, where he was wealthy and honored. Dismayed by the corruption and inefficiency that had taken root in the Portuguese colony in India, King João III, who had taken the Portuguese throne on Manoel's death in 1521, appointed Gama viceroy there in 1524. Gama accepted the position, but his viceroyalty was a brief one; he died in Cochin on December 24, 1524. His body was brought back to Portugal and interred in a marble tomb in the church of São Jeronimo in Lisbon.

In 1542, Portuguese ships reached China, and the emperor allowed them to establish a trading post. The following year, Portuguese traders headed for China were blown off course and landed in Japan, thereby becoming the first Europeans to set foot in that island kingdom. These accidental discoverers were soon followed by Portuguese merchants and missionaries, each in their own way eager to establish themselves in Japan. For nearly a century Portugal earned an enormous profit as the middleman in the trade between China and Japan, swapping Chinese silk for Japanese silver and taking a commission from both sides. In 1557, Portugal established a large, permanent colony at Macao, on the southern coast of China, which became the headquarters of its activity in the Far East.

By the mid-16th century Portugal had grown rich on the spice trade (and its neighbor Spain had grown rich on the gold and silver of the Americas). The center of power in Europe had shifted from the Italian states of the eastern and central Mediterranean to the Iberian states of the Atlantic seaboard. In less than a century and a half from the time Prince Henry dispatched his first tentative expedition from Lagos, the tiny, insignificant country of Portugal had made itself the leading European imperial power in Asia.

The Convent of São Jeronimo in Lisbon provides a serene resting place for the restless mariner Vasco da Gama. As an explorer, Gama has been overshadowed by his contemporary Christopher Columbus, but Gama's first voyage constituted a greater feat of seamanship than did Columbus's discovery of the New World.

The Legacy
of Portugal

The Portuguese empire in the east was called the Estado da India, or State of India, and its capital was at Goa, where the viceroy lived. The rewards of empire were high: the historian G. V. Scammell reports that in the mid-15th century, on the threshold of Portugal's great expansion into Asia, the cost per ton of spices in Europe was 100 times greater than the cost per ton of a brand-new ship. Merchants and kings alike thought it worth spending a few ships, or a few hundred men, to bring home a cargo more precious than gold. King Manoel of Portugal certainly thought so, and he also felt that the Crown, as the sponsor of Gama's voyage, should reap the rewards. In 1505 or 1506 he declared a royal monopoly on the spice trade, which meant that any Portuguese who wanted to buy, carry, or sell spices had to purchase a license to do so from the king, who took a share of the profits.

Portugal's overseas empire reached its greatest extent in the mid-16th century, a few decades after Gama's epochal voyage. By that time Portugal owned a series of fortified trading posts along the east coast of Africa and the west and east coasts of India and also controlled the Indian Ocean island of Ceylon, now called Sri Lanka, as well as Hormuz, Malacca, the Spice Islands, and Macao. It had a base in Japan and had established a foothold in Brazil. On the outskirts of the empire, Portuguese adventurers and missionaries had penetrated lands as remote and mysterious as Vietnam and Tibet.

The profits from the spice trade with the Indies made Manoel the Fortunate's Portugal the wealthiest nation in Europe.

Despite Portugal's vaunting ambition and its undeniable success in opening the seaway to Asia, the Estado da India never became a unified, centrally controlled colonial state. Portugal was a small country, with a small population, and the Portuguese were simply spread too thinly over too much territory in Asia for them to maintain effective control for a long period of time. Many men were lost to shipwreck, fever and tropical disease, or war; by 1610 Portugal had only about 6,000 seamen around the world—too few to man its vessels.

For the same reason, the Portuguese always remained a very small minority in their foreign holdings. With a few exceptions, such as Macao, Portugal did not establish large residential colonies overseas. It sent out not settlers and families but soldiers, traders, and missionaries. Furthermore, the Portuguese abroad faced formidable opposition from three sources—the Arab merchants who had dominated the Indian Ocean trade before the arrival of the Portuguese; the native peoples of the Indies and their Muslim allies; and the other European powers, which resented Portugal's intrusion into the spice trade and its newfound grandeur. Before long, the Estado da India was under attack.

The Chinese, Malay, Indian, and Arab traders soon found new routes across the Indian Ocean, enabling them to bypass the Portuguese trading centers and tax collectors. By the 1560s much of the spice trade was being carried by Arab ships and caravans in and around the Red Sea rather than by Portuguese vessels rounding the Cape of Good Hope.

In 1570 the Muslim peoples of the Indies united in an attack on the Estado da India and seized the island of Ternate, in the Moluccas, from Portugal. Then the Ottoman (Turkish) Empire, which controlled the upper ends of the Red Sea and the Persian Gulf, made a foray into the Indian Ocean in 1585–86 and drove the Portuguese away from many of their East African strongholds, although

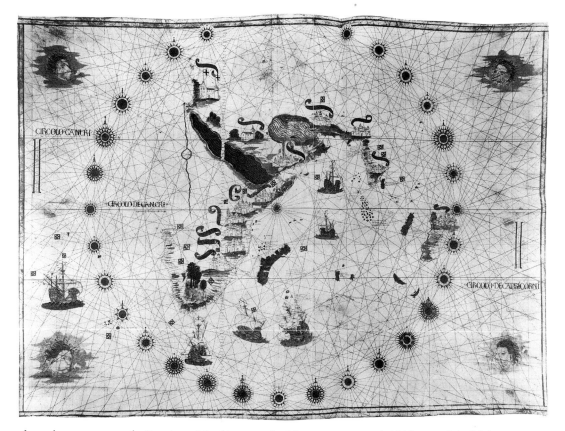

they later returned. Iranian Muslims took Hormuz in 1622. In the mid-17th century, Japan banned trade with Europeans and expelled the Portuguese. At about the same time, the Arab warlords of Oman, on the southeastern fringe of the Arabian Peninsula, went on the attack. By 1650 they had driven the Portuguese out of the Persian Gulf region, and by the 1670s they were harassing Portugal's bases in western India. The Maratha dynasty of Hindu rulers came close to conquering Goa in 1683.

The nations of Europe also began encroaching on Portugal's Asian territory. Spain, which generally approached the Indies from the Pacific Ocean, had established a secure base in the Philippines by the middle of the 16th century. In the 17th century, France set up posts on Madagascar and acquired trading rights from the rulers of some

A 1510 map of the Moluccas, or Spice Islands, which are today part of Indonesia. In the person of Francisco Serrão, the Portuguese at last reached the Spice Islands, which were the world's greatest producers of nutmeg and cloves, in 1513.

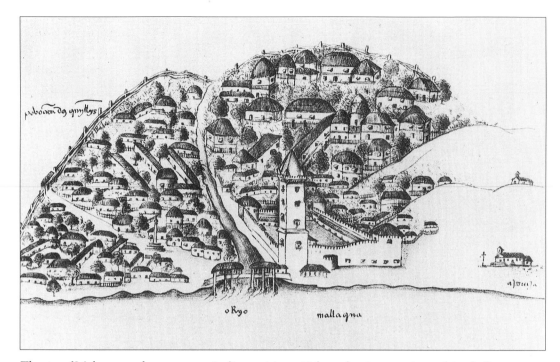

poboaca dg gyytlys
o Ryo   *mallagna*   *a)oua)a*

The city of Malacca, on the east coast of the Strait of Malacca near the southern end of the Malay Peninsula, was the entrepôt for much of the trade in spices from the Moluccas. It fell to Albuquerque and the Portuguese in 1511.

Indian cities. Other foreign nations hired Portuguese seamen to serve as navigators in order to learn the secrets of the *carreira da India*, as the voyage from Portugal to India and back was called. The greatest challenges came from Britain and the Netherlands. Britain's East India Company (EIC) was founded in 1600, and the British quickly found allies among Indian princes who hated the Portuguese. When Britain and Portugal became allies for a time as a strategic check on Spain, the British established a colony at Bombay on India's Malabar Coast. The British poured vast sums of money into the EIC, and soon the British greatly outnumbered the Portuguese in India. By the 18th century, Goa was Portugal's last Indian holding.

The Netherlands also established an East Indian trading company, but it focused on the Spice Islands of present-day Malaysia and Indonesia. With a large, disciplined navy and substantial financial support from the merchant community at home, the Dutch took Malacca in 1641, Sri Lanka in 1658, and several Malabar Coast ports in the

1660s. Before the end of the 17th century, Indonesia had become a Dutch colony; by 1700 the Indies trade belonged almost entirely to the British and the Dutch, and the Estado da India was a thing of the past.

In his *Grammatica*, published in 1539–40, Portuguese historian João de Barros wrote:

> The Portuguese arms and commemorative pillars placed in Africa and Asia, and in so many thousand islands beyond the three continents of the world, are material things, and Time may destroy them. But Time will not destroy the religion, the customs, and the language which the Portuguese have implanted in these lands.

Barros was right. The wooden crosses rotted, and the stone padrões crumbled, but the Portuguese influence lingers on in virtually every place touched by Portugal's seafaring mariners and merchants. The Madeira and Azores islands remain part of Portugal. The Cape Verdes belonged to Portugal until 1975, when they became an independent nation. Goa stayed a Portuguese possession until it was made part of India in 1962. Macao is still an overseas province of Portugal. All of these places share a Portuguese ethnic heritage, the Portuguese language, and the Roman Catholic religion.

The Portuguese presence remained strong in West Africa until the 20th century. The nation of Angola was formerly a Portuguese colony and then an overseas province of Portugal; it attained independence in 1975. Portuguese is still its official language. On the east coast of Africa, the nation of Mozambique also belonged to Portugal until 1975; there, too, Portuguese is still spoken. The architecture, institutions, and religion of these countries reflect centuries of Portuguese colonial rule.

Portugal exerted its most extensive and lasting influence on Brazil, which remained its largest overseas colony until achieving its independence in 1822. The Portuguese heritage is more evident there than anywhere else outside

Portugal. Brazil is the world's largest Catholic nation and the largest Portuguese-speaking nation.

Slavery is another legacy of Portugal's seaborne empire that shaped today's world. The institution of slavery is as old as human history, but by transporting blacks from West Africa, Portugal inaugurated the modern era of large-scale slave trading. Like the other imperial powers of Europe, Portugal took slaves in all parts of the world, capturing them by force or buying them from local warlords or dealers. The shipping of hundreds of thousands of blacks from Portuguese territories in Africa to the New World had profound consequences, giving rise to a long and tragic history of racial oppression, rebellion, and conflict.

For more than 100 years, from the mid-15th to the mid-16th century, tiny Portugal was the world's foremost seafaring nation. Inspired by Prince Henry, the Portuguese launched a series of voyages that changed the world. The Portuguese navigators introduced new techniques and instruments that would be adopted by the mariners of other nations; they pioneered sea routes that others would follow. While Spain opened up a New World for Europe—quite by accident—Portugal concentrated on finding new ways to traverse the known world; and in their immediate consequences Portugal's discoveries were even more momentous, resulting in a shifting of Europe's focus away from the Mediterranean toward the broader oceans. Indeed, it was Portugal's example that inspired the voyages of exploration of Columbus and Spain's other mariners that so changed the course of history.

The contributions of the earliest Portuguese navigators have sometimes been overlooked, but each voyage built upon those that had preceded it—there would have been no Gama without Gil Eanes. The voyages of Tristão, Cão, and Dias, like the later voyages of Columbus and Magellan, filled in blank spaces on the maps and in the minds of people who were becoming increasingly curious about their world. Finally, the voyage of Vasco da Gama opened

A battle at Gujarat, north of Bombay in India, between the Portuguese and the Arabs, who were determined to protect their trade monopoly in the region. Insufficient manpower would prove a severe hindrance to Portugal's ability to maintain its Asian empire.

This engraving was based on a painting by the French artist Jean-Honoré Fragonard, who in turn drew his inspiration from Os Lusíadas, *the epic poem of Portugal's seafaring men written by Luiz Vaz de Camões.* "And if there had been more of the world," *wrote Camões, "they would have reached it."*

the way for the influx of Europeans into Asia and Africa, a clash of cultures that continues to echo today. In the course of their search for spices, gold, and nonexistent Christian kings, the Portuguese navigators set off a centuries-long drama of interaction, colonization, and revolution that touched nearly every part of the globe. Their finest memorial is Portugal's epic poem *Os Lusíadas* (The Sons of Portugal), by Luiz Vaz de Camões, which was published in 1572. Beginning with Gama's first voyage to India, *Os Lusíadas* celebrates the giants of Portugal's age of exploration. "This is the story of heroes who, leaving their native Portugal behind them, opened a way to Ceylon, and further, across seas no man had ever sailed before," it begins.

Further Reading

Boorstin, Daniel J. *The Discoverers: A History of Man's Search to Know His World and Himself*. New York: Random House, 1983.

Boxer, Charles R. *The Portuguese Seaborne Empire, 1415–1825*. New York: Knopf, 1969.

Cameron, Ian. *Magellan and the First Circumnavigation of the World*. New York: Saturday Review Press, 1973.

Correa, Gaspar. *Three Voyages of Vasco da Gama*. New York: Franklin, Burt, 1964.

Divine, David. *The Opening of the World*. New York: Putnam, 1973.

Forbath, Peter. *The River Congo*. New York: Harper & Row, 1977.

Hart, Henry H. *Sea Road to the Indies: An Account of the Voyages & Exploits of the Portuguese Navigators, Together with the Life and Times of Dom Vasco da Gama, Capitão-Mor, Viceroy of India & Count of Vidigueira*. Westport, CT: Greenwood Press, 1950.

Jones, Vincent. *Sail the Indian Sea*. London: Gordon and Cremonesi, 1978.

Morison, Samuel Eliot. *The Great Explorers: The European Discovery of America*. New York: Oxford University Press, 1978.

Pennington, Piers. *The Great Explorers*. London: Bloomsbury Books, 1979.

Ravenstein, E. G., ed. and trans. *A Journal of the First Voyage of Vasco da Gama, 1497–1499*. London: Hakluyt Society, 1898.

Rogers, Francis M. *The Quest for Eastern Christians: Travel and Rumor in the Age of Discovery*. Minneapolis: University of Minnesota Press, 1962.

Sanderlin, George William. *Eastward to India*. New York: Harper & Row, 1965.

Scammell, G. V. *The First Imperial Age: European Overseas Expansion, c. 1400–1715*. London: Unwin Hyman, 1989.

Stanley, Henry E. J., ed. and trans. *The Three Voyages of Vasco da Gama and His Viceroyalty: From the Lendas da Indies of Gaspar Correa*. London: Hakluyt Society, 1869.

Stefoff, Rebecca. *Ferdinand Magellan and the Discovery of the World Ocean*. New York: Chelsea House, 1990.

———. *Marco Polo and the Medieval Explorers*. New York: Chelsea House, 1992.

Wilford, John Noble. *The Mapmakers*. New York: Knopf, 1981.

Zurara, Gomes Eanes de. *The Chronicles of the Discovery and Conquest of Guinea*. Edited and translated by C. Raymond Beazley and Edgar Prestage. London: Hakluyt Society, 1896.

Chronology

1341	Three ships sent by King Afonso IV visit the Canary Islands
1419–20	Captains under the command of Prince Henry discover the Madeira Islands
1420s	Gonçalo Velho Cabral discovers the Azores
1441	Nuno Tristão reaches Cape Blanco in present-day Mauretania; Antão Gonçalves brings the first black slaves from the West African coast to Portugal
1444	Portuguese mount the first European slave-taking expedition to West Africa; Dinís Dias reaches Cape Verde, the westernmost point of Africa
1446	Tristão passes the mouth of the Gambia River; killed in a skirmish with natives
1457	Alvise da Cadamosto reaches the Cape Verde islands and claims them for Portugal
1460	Pedro de Sintra reaches the coast of present-day Sierra Leone; Henry dies at Sagres
1469	King Afonso V leases exploration rights along the African coast to Fernão Gomes, who over the next five years extends Portugal's knowledge of the coast 2,000 miles southward
1482	Diogo Cão reaches the mouth of the Congo River in present-day Zaire
1487–88	Pero da Covilhã sets out on a mission of reconnaissance to India by way of the Persian Gulf; Bartolomeu Dias succeeds in rounding the southern tip of Africa
1493	Christopher Columbus returns from his first voyage to the Americas; Covilhã arrives in Abyssinia
1494	The Treaty of Tordesillas, promulgated by Pope Alexander VI, divides the newly discovered lands between Spain and Portugal
1497–99	Vasco da Gama reaches India via the Cape of Good Hope, establishing the long-sought eastern route to the Indies

1500	En route to India, Pedro Álvares Cabral discovers and claims Brazil for Portugal; other Portuguese mariners visit Greenland and Newfoundland
1501–2	João da Nova discovers the islands of Ascension and St. Helena in the South Atlantic Ocean
1502–3	Gama makes his second voyage to India; uses brutal means to establish Portuguese trade presence and crush opposition of local rulers
1505	Francisco de Almeida becomes viceroy of India
1506	Tristão da Cunha discovers islands in the South Atlantic and explores Madagascar
1510	Afonso de Albuquerque, the new viceroy of India, conquers Goa, which becomes the seat of Portuguese power in Asia
1511	Albuquerque conquers Malacca, an important trading city near present-day Singapore
1515	Portuguese forces gain control of the Strait of Hormuz in the Persian Gulf
1519–22	Spanish fleet under the command of Portuguese navigator Ferdinand Magellan makes the first circumnavigation of the world
1524	Gama made viceroy of India; dies at Cochin on December 24
1542	Portuguese merchants establish trading posts on the coast of China
1543	Portuguese traders blown off course become the first Europeans to land in Japan
1557	Portugal establishes the colony of Macao
1572	Publication of Portugal's *Os Lusíadas*, by Luiz Vaz de Camões, which begins with an account of Vasco da Gama's voyage to India and celebrates the heroes of Portugal's great age of exploration and expansion

Index

Picture Credits

Arguivo Nacional de Torre do Tembo, Lisbon, Portugal (Gaspar Correia "Lendas da India," *Meandos do Seculo XVI*): pp. 24, 100; Courtesy of The Bettmann Archive: pp. 18, 20, 26, 34, 36, 38, 39, 43, 44, 47, 60–61, 65, 73, 74, 75, 82, 94, 95; Courtesy Bibliothèque Nationale, Paris: p. 23; The Folger Shakespeare Library: p.56; Herzog August Bibliothek, Wolfenbüttel, Germany: p. 99; Vikki Leib (map): p. 57; Courtesy of the Library of Congress: pp. 12, 14, 17, 40, 62, 70, 80, 86, 88, 89, 92, 93, 103; New York Public Library: pp. 31, 77, 91, 97; Pierpont Morgan Library: p. 30; Courtesy of the Portuguese Embassy: pp. 49, 52–53, 67; Print Collection, Miriam and Ira D. Wallach Division of Art, Prints and Photographs, New York Public Library, Astor, Lenox, and Tilden Foundations: pp. 28, 78; Courtesy of the Rare Books and Manuscripts Division, New York Public Library, Astor, Lenox, and Tilden Foundations: pp. 50–51, 51, 52, 54–55, 55; Weidenfeld and Nicholson, Ltd.: p. 102

Rebecca Stefoff is a Philadelphia-based freelance writer and editor who has published more than than 40 nonfiction books for young adults, including *Ferdinand Magellan and the Discovery of the World Ocean* and *Marco Polo and the Medieval Explorers* in the Chelsea House WORLD EXPLORERS series. Stefoff received her M.A. and Ph.D. degrees in English from the University of Pennsylvania, where she taught for three years.

William H. Goetzmann holds the Jack S. Blanton, Sr., Chair in History at the University of Texas at Austin, where he has taught for many years. The author of numerous works on American history and exploration, he won the 1967 Pulitzer and Parkman prizes for his *Exploration and Empire: The Role of the Explorer and Scientist in the Winning of the American West, 1800–1900*. With his son William N. Goetzmann, he coauthored *The West of the Imagination*, which received the Carr P. Collins Award in 1986 from the Texas Institute of Letters. His documentary television series of the same name received a blue ribbon in the history category at the American Film and Video Festival held in New York City in 1987. A recent work, *New Lands, New Men: America and the Second Great Age of Discovery*, was published in 1986 to much critical acclaim.

Michael Collins served as command module pilot on the *Apollo 11* space mission, which landed his colleagues Neil Armstrong and Buzz Aldrin on the moon. A graduate of the United States Military Academy, Collins was named an astronaut in 1963. In 1966 he piloted the *Gemini 10* mission, during which he became the third American to walk in space. The author of several books on space exploration, Collins was director of the Smithsonian Institution's National Air and Space Museum from 1971 to 1978 and is a recipient of the Presedential Medal of Freedom.